WILLIAM 'JOCK' DAVIDSON

William 'Jock' Davidson has a record as a house plant specialist which few can equal. He has been growing, showing and talking about these plants for more than 30 years – ever since he left the Royal Air Force in 1947 and joined Rochford's, the company which pioneered the production of house plants in Great Britain.

Today he is a director of the company and is responsible for staging their superb exhibits at major flower shows all over the country. He was made an Associate of Honour of the Royal Horticultural Society in 1977 for his achievements in this area of gardening.

He is known to a wide public through his broadcasts on television and radio, his lectures, books and other writings. A Scot from Wick in Caithness, he is also known for his dry sense of humour and his philosophy that growing house plants should be fun.

'JOCK' DAVIDSON'S HOUSE PLANT BOOK

WILLIAM DAVIDSON

Line drawings by Constance Marshall

Hamlyn Paperbacks

'JOCK' DAVIDSON'S
HOUSE PLANT BOOK
ISBN 0 600 34599 8

First published in Great Britain 1980
by Hamlyn Paperbacks
Copyright © by William Davidson 1980

Hamlyn Paperbacks are published by
The Hamlyn Publishing Group Ltd,
Astronaut House,
Feltham,
Middlesex, England

Set, printed and bound in Great Britain by
Cox & Wyman Ltd, Reading

CONTENTS

	Introduction	vii
Chapter One	**House Plant Consultant**	1
Chapter Two	**Making a Start**	10
Chapter Three	**Davidson's Dozen**	17
Chapter Four	**The Right Plant in the Right Place**	27
Chapter Five	**Perfect for Presents**	51
Chapter Six	**Stop, You're Killing Me!**	61
Chapter Seven	**Raising Plants and Keeping Them Happy**	74
Chapter Eight	**Quick-check Guide**	83
Chapter Nine	**Davidson's File**	101
Chapter Ten	**The Future is Already Here**	185
	Index	193

INTRODUCTION

Why 'Jock' Davidson, when the man was christened William Davidson is a good question. I suppose that it is just one of those things for there has always been much confusion over whether I am Bill, Jock, or William.

But whatever the reason for the name, it has taken me into many odd corners in my efforts to popularise house plants – either by writing about them, displaying them, or more especially, by talking about them (for which the venue can be a village hall, the grand hall of a London teaching hospital, or a chair in a broadcasting studio).

Supporters of the fund raisers for a hospital were holding an evening entertainment some years ago at which I was to speak to a paying audience on the subject of potted plants. The charming professor seemed most anxious at the dinner which preceded the lecture to ascertain that my name was in fact William Davidson, and that my friends called me Jock. Several times I had to confirm that I really was William, but better known as Jock. The reason for his concern to get the facts right became apparent when, as chairman of the meeting, he opened the proceedings and finished up by introducing me with the words, 'And tonight we have with us Mr Willliam Davidson, who says his friends refer to him as Jock. Of course, you will all know that in the hospital we have our own Professor William Davidson, who hails from Aberdeen.' Then with a devilish chuckle, he added, 'I can't imagine anyone going up to him and calling him Jock!' The thought of anything so unlikely quite made his day, and we had a splendid evening.

By strange coincidence, there was in the audience that same evening a woman out-patient who had been attending the hospital for some years with a nervous disorder. And it would seem that my approach to house plants – that growing them should be an enjoyable pastime – made quite an impression on the lady in question. Meeting her and her husband at the Chelsea Flower Show some two years later, her husband said that my talk had done more good for her nervous condition than any medical treatment she had undergone. It seems that instead of a nervous complaint she had a house full of potted plants (two hundred, no less), and she could not find enough hours in the day to look after them. Her husband was delighted with the change, and his only real problem was in finding someone whom his wife could thoroughly rely upon to care for the plants while they were absent from home.

Although we cannot guarantee to cure everyone with a nervous problem, the lady's reaction to the soothing presence of plants in the home indicates that they can be much more than decorative features. I must admit, too, that they can sometimes have the reverse effect, being frustrating and difficult enough to bring on nervous disorders in the person who is caring for them, and cause more biting of finger nails with every leaf that drops and every greenfly that settles on a leaf.

Seriously, though, I feel that looking after plants indoors should be a pleasurable activity, and hope that what I have to say here will help to make it so.

CHAPTER ONE

House Plant Consultant

Although I am not a paid consultant, in the recognised sense, I am at the mercy of everyone who ever goes to a major flower show, as a man with a badge on his chest who does his duty in and around the exhibition. I am also responsible for replying to countless letters concerning the plight of Rubber Plants, non-flowering saintpaulias and such like. But perhaps the most interesting aspect of the consultancy work I do is the radio programmes during which questions are asked and I have no idea what they are going to be until they actually ring in my ear.

I get terrible vibrations when presented with dilapidated plants that my magic words are, hopefully, going to revive. Meeting someone at a flower show who obviously has something to show me turns me cold because by the time he or she has plucked up sufficient courage to bring it along, the plant is usually beyond recovery. The specimen has often travelled many miles and has perhaps been in a polythene bag for 24 hours or more, with the result that by the time I set eyes on it, it is a decomposed and smelly mess.

As he (or she) begins to open the bag of decaying vegetation other visitors crowd around to see what is going on. We look in the bag and a voice coyly mutters 'What do you think is wrong with it?'

In my position of adviser I am looking at the pulpy mess in the bag (I dare not touch it), and I'm thinking to myself, 'What in the hell is it?'

But the simple question cannot be asked, not with everyone waiting for my learned prognostication. So it is a matter of hedging, chatting around the subject for a bit; and in due course I usually discover that what the mysterious bag contains is an African Violet. Maybe one that was planted in the rock garden to give a bit of colour (a good phrase) on some remote hillside in North Wales! It does happen.

And I am suggesting now that if you want advice of this kind, don't wait until the plant is actually dead. Send – or post – something that the recipient can recognise; and rather than put it in a plastic bag it is often better to place it between two sheets of blotting paper sealed in a fairly strong envelope. The plant material will not then decompose quite so rapidly.

So the flower show is one side of my consultancy scene. And if an African Violet in a rock garden seems incredible, what about the seemingly intelligent lady who brought a very dead and shrivelled plant for me to see. With a trained horticultural thumb I felt the surface of the soil and remarked that it was very dry. (My trained eye could see that the soil had shrunk away from the side of the pot through drought conditions, but for effect you have to use the thumb.)

The lady responded to my very dry remark with the startling comment that she watered the plant every day. I had no wish to argue so followed up with, 'How much water do you give it every day?'

I nearly lost my composure when she replied very succinctly 'Three drops.' (This was Chelsea Flower Show, not the Victoria Palace.) By now a crowd had gathered and was listening intently as, ever more fascinated, I asked her why she only gave it three drops.

I had to swallow hard when she replied 'I give it one for the Father, one for the Son, and one for the Holy Ghost.'

After such experiences how can one remain too serious about house plants all the time! But it also brings up the question which is frequently asked – 'How do I water my plant?' Ideas on how this should be done vary greatly, and my feeling is you should well water the plant, see the water actually drain through into the reservoir at the base of the container that will catch the surplus, and allow the plant to dry out reasonably before watering it again. To be continually watering the vast majority of plants is detrimental to them. But there are exceptions, and these are covered in my advice on specific plants in Chapter Nine.

Besides attending flower shows, doing radio programmes, and replying to countless readers' letters, I am frequently to be found standing up before an audience of horticulturists, or others interested in the subject of house plants. We meet the lady or gentleman who is the finest potted cyclamen grower for miles around – the one who wins all the prizes at the shows. The questioner having gathered sufficient courage to stand up and put a question at the meeting, tells us the secret of his or her success. First the plants are grown on the kitchen window-sill where they have good light (my experience of talking to people at flower shows and elsewhere suggests that the kitchen windowsill is where all the better plants are grown indoors). There then follows what is thought to be the real secret behind their cyclamen-growing success – cold tea! All the plants are watered with cold tea – everyone in the room laughs at this and lots of them are obviously thinking, 'Poor soul.'

But I meet many people who grow their plants successfully by this method, and cold tea is an excellent liquid with which to water all indoor plants as it is nothing more than water with the chill taken off it which has also had all the impurities boiled away.

Another dear old lady grows the most marvellous African Violets. The secret of her success is that she goes around and gently blows on each one every night before putting the lights out and going to bed. If anybody went through this exercise on a plant nursery they would be looked upon with some concern, but in a room behind closed doors it does no harm.

Again perhaps we should not be over-facetious – there may, just possibly, be something in one's breath that does wonders for plants, though some of my Scottish acquaintances could quite easily kill off an African Violet at several paces with this treatment!

Sometimes we growers of plants ask for trouble, and we get it. Some years ago it became the practice to incorporate poly-styrene granules in potting compost, a practice which still continues, the idea being that the spongy little balls of poly-styrene help to keep the compost open, for the granules never break down as other ingredients do in the soil. Now, when plants are watered it is almost inevitable that some of these small white granules are going to find their way to the surface of the soil and remain there for all to see. Mrs Jones purchases her pot of ivy, or whatever it may be, in all innocence and takes it home only to find these strange things – growing perhaps, crawling, spreading, or could they be seeds?

A correspondent wrote to say she had bought a small pot of tradescantia and found that the soil was infested with strange things. Clearly there had been a break during the writing of the letter, as it continued in ink of a different colour and went on to say 'My friend has been. We have washed all the soil away from the roots to save them (ugh) and separated the seed from the soil. (They have now definitely become seeds, but worse is to follow.) My friend has a heated plant propagator and she has taken some of the seeds home to see if she can get them to germinate.' Oh dear!

One day I had a letter and inside the envelope another envelope containing a score of what appeared to be irregularly shaped green ball-bearings. The letter said that the writer had an orange tree which had been doing fine until very recently when these strange green things began to appear at the ends of the branches. He had, as he said, quite naturally taken the precaution of removing them and was now sending them to us for identification.

A PS to the letter said 'When can I expect my citrus tree to have the little oranges that you sometimes see on these plants?' My reply was very succinct – 'Never. You see, the little green things that you sent in the envelope were the baby oranges.'

Whether they are on radio programmes, come at the end of lectures or through the post, or even when I am standing minding my own business in the saloon bar of the local, many, many questions get put to me on house plants. Some of these recur time after time. Below are some typical questions with my reasonably typical answers. Much more detailed information on particular plants is given in Chapter Nine.

Question: Why is it that my saintpaulias are so reluctant to flower for a second time?

Answer: The usual reason for saintpaulias failing to flower indoors is because they are growing in positions that are poorly

4

lit. If they are to do well, they must have the lightest possible windowsill on which to grow, with the proviso that they have some protection from very strong sunlight. They must also be given the benefit of growing underneath, or adjacent to, a table or wall lamp in the evenings.

Plants will very often come into flower if the soil is kept on the dry side. That does not mean to say that the plants should be allowed to become bone-dry to the point of shrivelling, but rather that there should be a slight reduction in the amount of water normally given. There is a further possibility, and that is that many of the house plant fertilisers that are used are very high in nitrogen, which results in plants fed with them producing much more lush foliage, very often at the expense of flowers. When you have flowering plants to care for, I suggest that you should consult your house-plant supplier and let him provide you with a fertiliser that has a higher potash content.

Question: Why do the leaves on my Rubber Plant turn brown and fall off?

Answer: As Rubber Plants get older and the lower part of the stem turns a dark brown in colour then it is not unnatural for them to shed their lower leaves. However, when younger plants shed lower leaves in this fashion it is almost invariably an indication that the soil in the pot is much too wet and that the roots are beginning to die off. The consequence of this is that the leaves are eventually going to turn brown and in time fall off. Leaves may also be lost as a result of growing plants in rooms that are much too hot. The Rubber Plant should enjoy reasonably cool conditions in order to do well. And it will also be detrimental to plants if they are grown in poor light conditions.

Question: Will it harm my monstera plant if I remove the long roots that appear from the main stem?

Answer: It will not harm a well-established plant if a percentage of these aerial roots are removed, but one should not be too severe when performing this operation. I would suggest that it would be much better to tie the roots in carefully to the main stem of the plant, and when they are long enough they should be directed into the soil from which they can obtain moisture and nourishment.

Question: Why does my monstera plant produce small complete leaves rather than the attractive cut-out leaves that one normally sees?

Answer: The simple answer to this is that the plant is growing in a position where it is not getting sufficient light. Although monsteras do not need to be in full sunlight they do require a reasonable amount of light in order to do well and produce more attractively cut-out leaves.

Question: I am often at a loss to know how I should set about pruning some of my house plants, especially the overgrown ones.

Answer: The simple answer to this is that foliage plants, such as nephthytis and philodendron, can be pruned at almost any time. However, flowering plants such as beloperone or Shrimp Plant should only be pruned when the plant stops producing colourful flowers (bracts, in this instance). What you should do is simply to cut back the plant until it has a more attractive shape, and make the cuts immediately above a leaf joint.

Question: Why does my hibiscus plant shed flowers, and very often shed buds before they open?

Answer: This has become a very frequent question in recent years, as the hibiscus has increased in popularity. The reason hibiscuses shed buds and flowers is again a question of light. If they do not get sufficient light, then buds and flowers will either not develop at all, or they will drop off before they are fully mature. Buds and flowers on the side of the plant that is away from the light source will very frequently fail to open, or be much less in evidence.

Question: My *Hedera canariensis* has developed very brown and dry-looking leaves. Can you please prescribe the correct treatment?

Answer: This condition usually results from an attack by red spider mites, and when the leaves turn brown and dry as described they also develop a tendency to turn inwards. The action to take is to thoroughly spray the plant, especially on the undersides of the leaves, and to get some advice from your plant shop as to which insecticide to use. There is an ample range of these to choose from.

Question: When and how do I pot my plants?

Answer: A very good question. I suggest that you only pot plants that are healthy and have a well-established root system. This does not mean just a few wispy roots appearing through the holes in the bottom of the pot; it means that there should be a well-matted system of roots showing through the soil ball when you remove the plant from its pot. The size of the pot or other container used when repotting should be only a little larger than the one the plant is already growing in at the time. It is also advisable when potting plants to make sure that you use a properly prepared potting mixture and not garden soil, unless you have really superb soil in your garden. There are further notes on this subject on p. 78.

Question: Can I put my plants out in the garden during the summer months?

Answer: Yes, but I would suggest that they should be placed in a shaded place that is also sheltered from the prevailing wind. They must also be given just as much attention in respect of watering and feeding as they would have been given if they had been left indoors. I have more to say about this on p. 42.

Question: What should I do with my Bromeliad plants after they have flowered?

Answer: When a flower is no longer attractive, it should be completely removed, and when the rosette from which the flower has emerged loses its attractive appearance it, too, should be cut away, so allowing the young shoots at the base of the plant to grow up more naturally and more freely. If one

7

has a mind to, these young shoots can be removed and planted up individually, but it will extend the time that the shoots take to produce flowers on their own.

Question: What can I do with my plants when I am on holiday?

Answer: I would suggest that the best thing to do is to take the plants to a willing neighbour, or better still, if you are on friendly enough terms with a neighbour, then allow him or her to come into the house and deal with the plants *in situ*. This arrangement has many advantages: it avoids the set-back that plants can suffer when subjected to a different environment, and your house will have a lived-in look during your absence – which can be very important. There are other alternatives if this is not possible, and I discuss this matter in more detail in Chapter Six (see p. 67).

Question: There are lots of black sooty marks on my citrus plant. What action should I take?

Answer: Numerous plants are affected by black, sooty mould as a result of aphids and scale insects attacking the plant. I would suggest that the affected leaves should be cleaned with a damp sponge and that the plant be thoroughly sprayed with the appropriate insecticide.

Question: Can I divide some saintpaulia plants that have become very large and overgrown?

Answer: Yes, it is possible, but if the plants are very old and very full of leaves, then it is not advisable. With younger plants the roots can certainly be teased apart so that each section can be planted individually. But where older plants are concerned it is often best to remove a few leaves and propagate new, healthy, young plants from these (see p. 174) rather than attempt division.

Question: I cannot stop the ends of the leaves from browning on my chlorophytum. What am I doing wrong?

Answer: In my view it is almost impossible to grow chlorophytums in small pots that do not have brown tips to their leaves.

The reason for this is that they make very large fleshy roots that gather in the bottom of the pot, and, consequently, the plant is invariably slightly starved of nourishment. The problem could be overcome by repotting into ever-larger pots, but this is not always a practical proposition.

Question: I bought a polyanthus on Friday. But by Monday, although I treated it well, it looked like a two-week old lettuce – it had wilted completely. What is the matter with it?

Answer: I love that phrase 'like a two-week old lettuce'. I have seen so many dead and dying polyanthuses and primulas looking just like that! The only way to bring such a plant back to life is to take the pot in both hands, place your thumbs over the top of the soil and submerge the pot in a bucket of water until the bubbles cease to rise to the surface. This ensures that the plant has been thoroughly watered; and besides being the ideal treatment for primulas that look like 'two-week old lettuces', it is also the perfect way to water azaleas.

CHAPTER TWO

Making a Start

The first horse I ever backed came in at 33 to 1 – which could be termed beginner's luck, something arranged by the bookmaker so that he can get you in his net, perhaps. But my only bet now is on the Grand National, and I am seldom very successful.

The beginner with house plants will, in all probability, be much more successful (or lucky) if he lays his bets cautiously at the beginning and backs the easier rather than the exotic plants – for these last will surely prove to be 'non-runners', 'fallers-at-the-first-fence' or whatever the appropriate term may be. There will be time enough to grow the exotic calatheas and such like when you have acquired some skill with the easier plants. There are plenty of those that are interesting, colourful and exciting in their various ways.

The producer of house plants frequently gets into hot water with the dedicated house plant enthusiast, because he does not place sufficient emphasis on the proper botanical naming of his plants. But the grower has long since learnt that the vast majority of his customers are not desperately interested in plant nomenclature. What they want is an easily recognisable, preferably common name. I address many meetings throughout the year, and at many of these I will hold up a specimen of *Sansevieria trifasciata laurentii* and say, 'Does anyone know the name of this one?'

Fifteen years ago, such a question would have been received in dead silence as the majority of the audience averted their gaze (thinking, 'Horror of horrors, he's going to pick on me!') Nowadays, almost the entire audience will call out in unison, 'Mother-in-law's Tongue', while a few manage, or try to manage, its rather formidable botanical name. So, whatever may be said against common names (for example, that they frequently change from region to region – although not in this case – and are sometimes given to two quite different plants), there is little doubt that they provide the beginner with an easy way to become familiar with plants. There will be time enough later on to get to grips with botanical names.

To demonstrate the confusion which common names can cause, however, I would quote the case of the spider plant – the common name which most people associate with the grass-like *Chlorophytum comosum*. But one leading grower of house plants attaches the name of spider plant to *Aralia elegantissima*, which last, to add to the confusion, is synonymous with the name *Dizygotheca elegantissima*. The last-mentioned name is, in fact, the one currently valid, but is there any wonder that a grower should wish to hang on to the simpler name if he possibly can? After all, very ordinary people have to go into High Street flower shops and ask for these things by name – if they are not able to simply see the plant on a shelf and say, 'That's what my friend has. Can I have one please?'

However, to assist in an understanding of plant names, almost all botanical names have Greek or Latin roots and all plants are arranged in families, with the members of that family having certain characteristics in common. For example, all members of the spurge family, the *Euphorbiaceae* (different though they are in appearance), exude a milky sap when their tissue is damaged. Possibly the most important member of this family so far as the house plant grower is concerned is *Euphorbia pulcherrima*, which is better known as the colourful, Christmas-flowering Poinsettia.

Ficuses, for instance, belong to the *Moraceae* family and are many and varied in their appearance, from majestic trees to the creeping *Ficus pumila*. Ficus is the generic name (the equivalent of our surname) and is always written with a capital letter. There then follows the specific name (equivalent to our Christian name and having a small initial letter), which in the common Rubber Plant is *elastica* – thus, *Ficus elastica*. In recent years there have been two very important improvements in *F. elastica*; first *F. elastica decora* and, more recently, *F.*

elastica robusta. The third word represents a variety or form of the species.

The newcomer to house plants, if presented with a choice of all three of these ficuses, should choose *robusta*. *F. elastica* has narrow, more drooping leaves and is a much inferior plant which is seldom offered for sale these days. The variety *decora* is a much improved plant and was grown in vast quantities until about 10 years ago when the much stronger and more vigorous *robusta* appeared and has, more or less, taken over from the previous two.

Improvements of this kind come about as the result of crossing one plant with another so that a more vigorous strain results, or it may be a chance event with an established variety producing a more vigorous side growth, that was noticed by someone with an experienced eye. Cuttings would be taken from this and propagated, so that plants could be grown on and checked to see if they had superior qualities. If it was confirmed that a marked improvement existed, the plant would be given a varietal name and introduced to commerce – just as *F. elastica robusta* has been. Anyone raising and registering such a plant today can claim royalties on all cuttings produced throughout the world, so discovering new plants and varieties can be a lucrative business.

The first plant purchase can influence greatly the attitude of the newcomer to house plants. Some awful rubbish is offered for sale in the guise of house plants. These plants are grown cheaply, packed tightly on the greenhouse staging, with every intention of raising plants which can be sold cheaply. Spraying against pests, and diseases, watering, feeding, and carrying out the many other tasks that are necessary to produce quality plants is almost impossible under these conditions. The consequence is that plants become thin, drawn and inferior, but still good enough to be sold to the retailer who is looking for something cheap that can be put out on the pavement to catch the eye of the passer-by. For this kind of grower, the greatest ally is the paper sleeve which is universally used to hold such plants in transit so that only the more acceptable top part can be seen. Reputable nurseries use paper sleeves as protection, not as camouflage.

From the foregoing it will not be difficult for the beginner to understand that it is unwise to purchase plants that are wrapped in paper without inspecting them first. It is much easier not to buy a faulty plant than it is to take it home, then take it back to the shopkeeper and complain. Many of them are not at all happy about dealing with complaints – and one can understand this after seeing what some house plant purchasers are capable of doing to healthy plants in a surprisingly short space of time!

Signs of poor culture are brown leaves around the base of the plant, or missing leaves from larger plants such as ficus and monstera. Discoloured leaves with a hard, yellowish-brown appearance overall should be avoided like the plague, as this is frequently an indication that the plant is suffering from the effects of attacks by red spider mite. Where the attack is severe there may even be signs of minute webs where the leaf stalk joins the leaf.

Elsewhere, I have more to say on the subject of pests and diseases, but it seems to be appropriate to offer here a word of warning to the beginner concerning the purchase of pest-ridden plants, as pests will quickly transfer their attentions to other plants once they have been introduced to room conditions. Once you have got an infestation of red spider mite, mealy bug or scale insects, they can be extraordinarily difficult to get rid of, so why buy the things in the first place?

Different plants require, and are given, different conditions when they are growing in the greenhouse of the professional grower, so once they have been transferred to the home there has to be adjustment, as they gradually become accustomed to what is an entirely new way of life. Therefore, it is important during the first few weeks that plants should not be neglected in respect of watering and feeding, and that plants bought in winter should be kept in a room with a reasonable temperature and be gradually acclimatised to cooler conditions.

But it should not be the aim of the beginner to grow exotic, high-temperature plants, and I would suggest as starters the following: *Chlorophytum comosum*; tradescantias in variety; *Rhoicissus rhomboidea*; *Philodendron scandens*, *Sansevieria trifasciata laurentii*; almost any member of the bromeliad family; *Monstera deliciosa*; *Hibiscus rosa-sinensis*; Christmas or Whitsun cacti (*Zygocactus truncatus* and *Schlumbergera gaertneri* respectively); and impatiens. These will give reasonable variety – some are tall-growing, some trailing and one or two have flowers to add a bit of colour to the scene.

In all walks of life, however, a challenge can be an exciting proposition, and with house plants the challenge can come when you feel you have mastered the art of growing the easy ones and want to move on to something more difficult. The following plants one might reasonably expect to do well indoors, provided they have that little bit of extra attention in the way of feeding, temperature and the like.

In fact, many of the so-called delicate plants settle down extraordinarily well in room conditions when there is an even temperature, for this is almost the most important requirement as far as such plants are concerned. For the majority, I would suggest that a minimum temperature in the region of 18.5°C. (65°F.) is ideal.

The dieffenbachia is one of the oldest established pot plants in the slightly more difficult sector, but it does surprisingly well in a room that is heated to this kind of temperature, and where there is good light but not necessarily exposure to full sun. Of the kinds available, *Dieffenbachia exotica* is without doubt the most popular, having cream and green leaf variegation. The majority of these plants are grown and sold in pots of 5in. (13cm.) size, and if you are lucky enough to buy a very large plant, it is advisable to pot it on into a slightly larger container almost as soon as you get it home. This can be a truly spectacular plant.

Another plant that has become increasingly popular is the codiaeum or Croton which is commonly called Joseph's Coat because of the many colours in the leaves. To do well and retain its leaf colour this plant needs to be grown in good light. It must also be provided with a reasonable temperature and the compost should never be allowed to dry out. Regular feeding is essential.

For more shady positions where the temperature is reasonably high, a wide selection of plants is available and particularly those grown for their foliage effects. Among these I would include almost all the ferns that you are likely to be able to buy, and most of the smaller marantas. The larger-leaved marantas tend to be much more difficult, and this also applies to the few calantheas that might be available.

The stately dracaenas in their many different forms are also very fine plants for a room with good light which is also reasonably well heated. Among these I would include *Dracaena terminalis*, *D. marginata* and *D. deremensis*. There is also *D. godseffiana* to consider – a much more compact plant with speckled green, gold and cream foliage. It is a much more tolerant plant that does well in less demanding conditions.

Another slightly more difficult flowering plant to consider is columnea. This has always been considered a delicate greenhouse plant but it is one that is well worth trying indoors in rather good conditions.

Among the flowering plants that are more difficult to manage I suppose one must include the saintpaulias, in spite of the fact that many people seem to be very successful in growing them nowadays. As mentioned elsewhere, it is important that saintpaulias should have good light in which to grow and a reasonable temperature, and it is advisable to water them with tepid water.

Some of the plants in your collection will become like old friends, almost part of the family in fact, and receive as much attention as the cat or dog.

One of my oldest plants is a battered old cactus that has been around for the best part of 25 years. It is commonly named Old Man Cactus, and, more properly, *Cephalocereus senilis*, and has suffered and flourished in all sorts of situations without giving up. It is still in a comparatively small 5in. (13cm.) pot, gets watered when I think about it during the spring and summer months and has nothing to drink from about October to March. Kept on a light windowsill, it would not win many prizes with its rather ungainly growth, but, as I've said, the old chap is like one of the family and the place wouldn't be the same without him.

A room without plants is like a new and empty greenhouse; both need filling with greenery without delay. But go about the business of stocking up in your own time and with your own choice of plants. There will be lots of friends who will be only too delighted to donate something to give you a start, and that could be your undoing. If you are given plants, make sure that they are healthy and good specimens to bring into the house.

If you are a beginner who is buying plants and you want to be lucky, the motto could be: 'Buy well to grow well'. And remember that you should at all times:

Anticipate the needs of your plants.

Watch out for pests and other troubles.

Make sure that your plants are given congenial atmospheric conditions.

Be tolerant while newly-bought plants are adjusting to the conditions they now find themselves in.

Feed your plants intelligently.

Water correctly – and always avoid over-watering.

Make arrangements for the care of your plants during holiday periods.

Make sure that you do not over-pot your plants.

CHAPTER THREE

Davidson's Dozen

Frequently I am asked what my favourite house plant is, and you might be interested to know which plants I would put in my favourite dozen. When you have worked with them for as long as I have, the problem is, of course, deciding what to eliminate. It is tempting to list the more difficult and exotic plants, but these are only likely to lead the reader to temptation – temptation that in the end would, in most instances, lead to costly disappointment as the acquired treasures wilt and die. There is also the added difficulty and frustration connected with finding a stockist and actually being able to buy the more unusual plants.

So there is a need to be realistic. Many of the plants I've chosen have been popular as house plants for many years, and there is no doubt that plants which have stood the test of time must have something going for them. Although *Hedera helix* Jubilee (syn. *H.h.* Gold Heart), which is one of my choices, is frequently in short supply, the other plants I've selected are generally available allowing, of course, for seasonal shortages in the case of the flowering plants. The care and attention needed by these plants is discussed in Chapter Nine.

Asplenium nidus
This fern is not top of the list simply because its name begins with the letter 'A'; it is there because well-grown plants in pots of about 7in. (18cm.) in diameter have no peers in the pot plant world. Their appearance is enhanced as the plants age, and growing perfect plants can be a daunting task, but the odd brown mark is usually acceptable. The pale green, almost translucent leaves are especially susceptible to physical damage,

and they will often be completely ruined if one is foolish enough to clean them with chemical leaf cleaners. New leaves must at no time be cleaned and older ones should only be cleaned with a soft sponge that has been soaked in water. The common name of Bird's Nest Fern for this plant presumably alludes to the shuttlecock arrangement of the leaves, which would clearly provide an excellent nest for the lazy bird once the appropriate nesting materials had been put in place!

Left to right: Hedera canariensis variegata (**Canary Island Ivy**), *Asplenium nidus* (**Bird's Nest Fern**) and *Ficus pumila* (**Creeping Fig**).

Ficus pumila

The Creeping Fig, as *Ficus pumila* is called, has many majestic relations in the huge fig family, many of which would seem to have prior claim to a place in Davidson's Dozen, but biggest is not necessarily best where plants and their appeal are concerned. The popularity of this simple little plant could well be a good enough reason for its inclusion here; but it has more to offer than that. It has the most beautiful pale green leaves which are oval in shape and attached to wiry and slender stems.

The plant has many uses as far as the arranger is concerned as the colouring and compactness of the foliage will provide the perfect low-growing foil for every sort of plant, no matter how garish their colouring may be. Warm, shaded conditions that are reasonably moist will suit it best, and occasional pinching out of the growing tips will ensure that the attractive, compact appearance is maintained. Although seen at its best in small pots, it will also be useful if several are grouped in shallow pans, or even in hanging baskets, but one must be sure not to neglect watering. Very dry conditions will inevitably result in the beautiful leaves quickly becoming crisp and dry.

Hedera canariensis variegata

Fancy, an ordinary ivy being included in a list of favourite plants! But, in spite of being grown by the million annually, *Hedera canariensis variegata* is still one of the finest of house plants. It is colourful, reasonably easy to grow and very adaptable. The leaves have a clearly defined white and green variegation, and the best plants are obtained by inserting several cuttings in a pot and growing them on. Although it may be grown as a trailer, the plant is most effective when trained to a single cane so that a tall, slender shape is achieved. It is adaptable in many respects, but the most important advantage is, perhaps, that it can be planted out of doors when it has outlived its usefulness in the home – or has lost its leaves as a result of being there!

Azalea indica

I must include the Indian azaleas (hybrid of *Azalea indica* or, if you want to be absolutely correct, *Rhododendron simsii*), if for no other reason than that I am among the fortunate band of pot plant enthusiasts who can grow this azalea on from one year to the next with little or no difficulty – much to the envy of my acquaintances. The woody stems and branches of this plant carry oval-shaped evergreen leaves that in themselves are not much to write home about, but these are crowned with an incredible profusion of flowers during the winter and spring months of the year. Flower colouring ranges from white to dark red with many fascinating shades and bicolors in between.

My home conditions for growing plants are very modest, and my azaleas are obliged to spend most of their non-flowering time out of doors, getting frost protection only, and this they appear to relish if results are anything to go by. In summer, plunge them in a bed of peat out of direct sunlight to reduce watering. Full sun will not be detrimental if you ensure that the potting mixture is never, repeat *never*, allowed to dry out. They must be brought back into the home before the first frosts of autumn arrive.

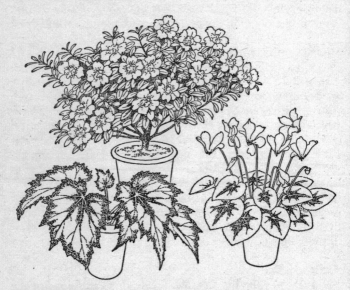

Bottom left, clockwise: Begonia rex, **an Indian azalea (hybrid of** *Azalea indica*) **and a florists' cyclamen (hybrid of** *Cyclamen persicum*).

Begonia

From this family one could well make up this total selection, be they flowering or foliage plants, or plants of general interest. Beautiful leaf markings characterise the *Begonia rex* varieties which, over the course of a few years, can make large plants. You will find that those with smaller leaves are the easiest to grow. The tendency the plants have to lose their lower leaves is a disadvantage and when this happens, rather unsightly rhizomatous stems tend to develop. Discarding the plants and starting again may be the best course to take. Certainly these none-too-easy plants are worth preserving with their handsome foliage effects. They need a room temperature in the region of 16°C. (60°F.) to do well, although it can be a few degrees less, and good light but not direct sunshine.

But now I must turn to a quite different kind of begonia. The tolerant plant that will flower over a very long period will frequently win favour, and that is so in the case of the fibrous-rooted *B*. 'Fireglow', which may also be seen sporting a number of other names on the label attached to the plant. *B*. Reiger is one of the names most often seen and the one that is more correct. Dark, glossy green leaves are borne on firm, fleshy stems that provide compact and attractive plants in a matter of months from the time the cuttings have rooted. The principal attraction, however, is the flowers that consist of clusters of single blooms on stalks that hold the heads of flowers just above the leaves. Vigorous plants will frequently become so floriferous that the leaves will be completely obscured.

At one time, red was the only colour available, and that is not the best colour for blending with the general run of foliage plants that come within the house plant range; but there are now many new shades that the flower and plant arranger will find much more adaptable to his needs. White is useful, but the pale salmons and delicate shades of yellow are exciting to use and more than kind on the eye. I find very often when displaying plants that I can get much better results by doing simple rather than complicated things. This is especially true with Fireglow, as it is set off to perfection when associated with a group of plants of the same colour in the same container. In a spacious entrance hall there is no more welcome sight than, say, three salmon-coloured flowered begonias plunged to their pot rims in moist peat, their colouring set off by a polished copper container. As plants increase in size it will be essential to provide thin supporting canes with their tops snipped off just below the topmost leaves. The canes must always be firm, neatly tied and unobtrusive if they are to do their important job effectively.

I've cheated a little by including two quite different begonias, and so making my overall selection a baker's dozen.

Cyclamen

The florist's cyclamen (hybrids of *Cyclamen persicum*) are tantalising plants, yet they never seem to fall off in popularity. For best results it would seem sensible to grow new plants from seed each year. Although they may be grown from year to year using the same corms, the sowing of seed will always be the more reliable method. Seeds germinate in warm conditions (about 16°C. [60°F.]) and, as leaves develop, so a hard corm forms in the centre of the pot; both flowers and leaves emerge directly from the corm, there being no main stems. If seeds are sown in August, the resulting plants will be in flower for Christmas of the following year, provided you keep the winter temperature above 10°C. (50°F.) and nearer 16°C. (60°F.) from the approach of flowering onwards.

The leaves are a cool grey-green in colour, with some of the more recent introductions having attractive silver variegation. The flowers are borne on stalks 1ft. (30cm.) or more in length, and generally form in a crowded group in the centre of the leaves. Their clean, fresh appearance is their chief attraction, and the wide range of colouring will suit almost every taste. As with Begonia Fireglow (see p. 21), quite startling effects can be achieved by grouping cyclamen in individual colours.

These cyclamen, however, have an alarming habit of seeming to curl up their toes and die for no apparent reason. This can frequently be traced to watering too heavily or, much more likely, to the fact that the plant is being subjected to temperatures that are excessive – cool conditions must ever be the aim if a quick exit to the dustbin is to be avoided.

Hedera helix Jubilee (syn. *H.h.* Gold Heart)

I am going to include another ivy, *Hedera helix* Jubilee when I know in my bones that I should be mentioning calatheas, pandanuses and things like that; but it is my choice and I am very fond of ivies – this one in particular. Jubilee is another ivy that does equally well out of doors; perhaps better than in the home if the superb specimen in my own garden is anything to go by. The leaf shape is typical of the smaller ivies, but the colouring of green with a rich golden centre is something very special and all its own. As an individual specimen on a single stem, it is superb, but it takes a long time to reach any size of consequence. Plants are reluctant to branch when the growing tip is removed so, to get a compact shape, it is necessary to wind the stems back and forth through the plant as it grows. Putting several cuttings in the pot to begin with is also essential.

Saintpaulia

The African Violet (saintpaulia) is high on my list. For those of us who are professionally concerned with house plants, there are few more rewarding things than to see in perfect African Violet plants the reward for one's efforts over many months of the year. T.L.C., tender, loving care, is often put forward as an essential need when growing saintpaulias indoors and, although the professional grower may cringe at the thought of applying these words to his efforts, they are equally relevant in the busy greenhouse. There is no margin for error with these plants – one night of low temperature, one watering (over leaves and flowers) with cold water and the T.L.C. of many months will be lost.

If the questions I get asked at shows or through the mail are anything to go by, it would seem that the saintpaulia is far and away the most popular of flowering pot plants. And this is probably due to the fact that they can be produced throughout the year by the professional grower, there being no special flowering season for them. Given good growing conditions and a varied selection of the many varieties which are available, plants can be had in flower all the year round.

Hibiscus cooperi variegata

I'm daft enough to believe that some plants actually know when there is a big event in the offing – and this could be one of them. With the brightest white and green (often tinged with pink) leaf variegation of any plant, *Hibiscus cooperi variegata*

23

will also produce, infrequently, trumpet-shaped red flowers. I have seen them at a three-day flower show produce one flower on each day – and nothing for weeks afterwards. Perhaps we do have a lot more to learn about them than we really think! Strong, woody stems develop in time, and a plant that is well cared for will make a magnificent specimen up to 8ft. (2.5m.) tall with a wealth of colourful foliage. Or, if preferred, it can be pruned so that a compact bush is the result. It is a really excellent plant for many locations, and one of my great favourites.

Bottom left, clockwise: **an African Violet (saintpaulia),** *Hibiscus cooperi variegata* **and** *Hedera helix* **Jubilee.**

Ananas bracteatus striatus

The fascinating Bromeliad family of plants all originate from the tropical regions of South America, and there are many fine examples that could well have found their way into this chapter, some with exotic foliage, others with colourful bracts, still others blessed with a happy combination of the two. The ananas, or Pineapple, is the only one that has any commercial value; all the others, large and small, are purely decorative. The green ananas of commerce is much less attractive, however, and I find it a very dull plant when compared with its variegated counterpart, *Ananas bracteatus striatus*. Plants form attractive rosettes of stiff recurving leaves that are viciously spined along the margin of the leaf, and are richly variegated. Older plants will in time produce pineapples on stout stems some 2ft. (60cm.) in length, and may then quite justifiably claim to be the most attractive of all potted plants. The spines along the margin of the leaf make them especially difficult plants to handle. I once met someone who was invited to visit the farm of an acquaintance in the tropics, only to regret that he had gone wearing a pair of shorts to what turned out to be a pineapple farm!

Monstera
One could select any number of plants from the *Araceae* family to fit into a favourite dozen, but few of them would match up

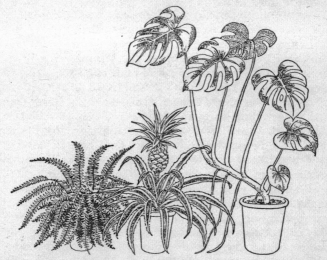

Left to right: Nephrolepis exaltata (**Ladder Fern**), *Ananas bracteatus striatus* (**variegated Pineapple**) and *Monstera deliciosa* (**Swiss Cheese Plant**).

25

to the all-round qualities of the Swiss Cheese Plant, *Monstera deliciosa*, which gets its common name from the way in which the leaves are deeply serrated along their margins and form the natural perforations that are said to resemble the holes in mature cheeses. The nurseryman raises almost all his plants from seed, and it takes some two years for the plants to develop their true characteristics – rich glossy green leaves with deeply indented margins – and in the region of a further two years before any quantity of perfectly symmetrical holes appear in the centre of the leaf. The inflorescence of the monstera is a rich creamy-white spathe with a central spadix and it remains but a few days before it fades and dies. From this stage it takes many months before the hard monstera fruit ripens and this, although unappetising in appearance, is delicious to eat – the reason, perhaps, for the name *deliciosa*. Monsteras have many other attractions and not least among them is the fact that they adapt very well to room conditions.

Nephrolepis

There are many varieties of *Nephrolepis exaltata* or Ladder Fern. They are often erroneously known by the common name of Boston Fern (a name that rightly belongs to *N. exaltata bostoniensis*), and are reminders of the Victorian days when, along with the aspidistra, they held pride of place in many an elegant drawing room. At their best as large plants, it is advisable to put several smaller plants into a 7in. (18cm.) pot and to keep them warm and humid until they have become established, when they will tolerate less demanding conditions. To display the plants effectively, they must have ample space around them, so it is wise to consider them as individual specimens and to place them on a pedestal, or you can get in on the hanging plant scene and suspend them from the ceiling so that they can be viewed from all angles. Many exhibitors at shows of my acquaintance would be like fish out of water if they did not have their 'nephros' to fit into all sorts of difficult corners when arranging their displays. They are really superb, indispensable plants.

CHAPTER FOUR

The Right Plant in the Right Place

One of the finest indoor plants I have ever seen was in the office of a typical 'all-go' executive and it had always occupied the same corner position in the room. He believed emphatically that once a plant had settled in and was obviously doing well, so it should remain. The plant was a specimen of *Dracaena godseffiana* Florida Beauty, which had broadly oval-shaped leaves that come to a point and with a colouring which is almost entirely rich yellow with odd splashes of green here and there.

It grew in a shallow, clay pan that was about 6in. (15cm.) in depth and some 2ft. (60cm.) in diameter. (Having grown limited numbers of this dracaena over many years, I have always found that it does best in this type of container.) There was good light, but no direct sunlight, the temperature never fell below 16°C. (60°F.) and it was an expensive plant to maintain. When the entire establishment closed down for the annual holidays, the other plants were taken to the nursery of the man who maintained them. But the dracaena had to remain, and the person looking after it had to make special twice-weekly visits to ensure that it was in good order.

There was no doubt about that. When I saw it, it was 8ft. (2.5m.) tall and very much better than any we had in our show greenhouse at the nursery. So here, most definitely, was the right plant in the right place: it had even temperature, good light, expert care and, most important to my mind, stability. Once it had found its niche it was left there to get on with it and not moved all over the place at the whim of its owner.

Moving some plants (indeed, just turning them round where they stand) can be detrimental; and this is especially so in respect of the Christmas and Whitsun cacti (*Zygocactus trun-*

catus and *Schlumbergera gaertneri* respectively), and the flowering hibiscus – all of which will shed buds and flowers if moved in this way. With smaller foliage plants less harm is done when the pots are rotated, and it can sometimes be an advantage to turn the pots so that growth is more evenly balanced. Almost all plants will grow towards, or turn their leaves towards, the light source in a room, which is proof of the fact that plants require good light in which to grow as a matter of high priority.

Many plants, including the caladium shown here, would be very unhappy left in the draught from an open door. Avoid such positioning.

Many plants will react very adversely to draughty conditions, and certainly if they are subjected to them over a prolonged period. Avoid positioning them near doors which will frequently be left open.

Sun Scorch Problems

When positioning plants, especially those with more tender

leaves, it is particularly important that they should not be exposed to direct sunlight. Frosted glass may not seem to allow as much light through as clear glass, but if the glass is of a flat, waved pattern, the rays of the sun are magnified considerably. Sun scorch then becomes a real problem, not only on tender leaves, but on the leaves of almost all plants. My tough old citrus plant suffered in this way, yet it is a plant that stands out of doors in full sun throughout the summer and never shows any sign of damage.

A monstera with sun-scorched leaves. Never place plants with tender leaves near windows, especially those fitted with frosted glass.

On very sunny days, plants that normally enjoy window positions will do all the better if they are taken into the room where they can have some protection. Or, if this is impractical, a sheet of newspaper placed between the plants and the glass will provide adequate protection. It may not be the most decorative of window adornments, but it works, and it is surprising what we plant lovers will do if we feel that the plant will benefit.

Frequent mention is made throughout this book of the need

to place plants in light window positions. It is one of those things I feel very strongly about, for plants need adequate light if they are to do well. But, and it is an important but, it is equally important that the same plants should be protected from very cold (or even moderately cold) conditions. This will mean taking them out of window areas when cold winter weather prevails, or at night when temperatures drop considerably. An oft-repeated warning is to ensure that plants are never left between the window pane and the curtains when the latter are drawn at nightfall, as the space between can become a very cold pocket of air which is harmful, if not indeed fatal, to many plants. It is also important that the leaves of plants should not actually touch the windowpane, as they will be more vulnerable to extremes of hot and cold conditions.

Using a Fireplace for Plants in Summer

Thinking of the undesirable homes that can be found for plants, this is an opportune time to mention the dangers to which plants placed in fireplaces during the summer months are exposed (a time, of course, when fires are not normally needed). Plants can be placed in a fireplace and look fine, if there is sufficient light for their needs, but the simple precaution that must be taken is to ensure that the chimney ventilator is blocked off so that plants are not harmed by draughts. A piece of firm cardboard cut to shape and wedged into position is all that is needed to offer adequate protection.

If that precaution is taken, the fireplace or hearth offers considerable scope as a home for house plants during the summer months of the year. It is the sort of area which can accommodate reasonably large containers without them being a nuisance by continually getting in the way. There are all sorts of modern containers available for this purpose, many of them quite hideous and totally unsuitable, but others – particularly those of copper colouring – fit the bill admirably. When buying such containers it is advisable to get something that will accommodate the full depth of a 5in. (13cm.) pot, which means in practice a depth of around 6in. (15cm.). Whether these containers take the form of troughs or bowls, they should be capable of holding a reasonable number of plants.

Trough-type containers are simple to arrange as all one has to do is set the plants in position. However, I would make the suggestion that you should place a layer of gravel in the bottom of the container before introducing the plant pots, for any surplus water that drains through when watering will lie in the bottom of the container but below pot level. This may appear a minor point, but it is essential to good growth that plants should not at any time stand with their pots in water. The soil becomes waterlogged and airless; the roots rot and die, and the

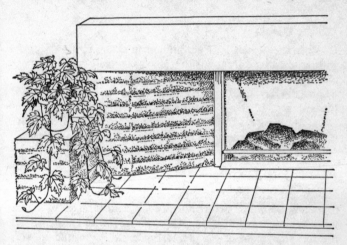

Rhoicissus **Ellendanica is one of the plants which could be used to brighten up a fireplace in summer.**

plant in time will follow suit. Deeper containers in which plants can appear 'lost' to view can also have gravel added so that the plants rest at their right level.

Gravel can also be used in circular containers, but in these it is possible to have much better plant arrangements by actually planting the root ball of the plant in soil or by plunging the pots in peat or moss. I favour moss as it is much cleaner to handle, and where it is exposed it is much more attractive. Use fresh sphagnum moss for this purpose, and either change it regularly or take the container out of doors and shake out the moss and leave it for a couple of days to let the air get at it. The reason for taking it out of doors is because moss, when disturbed, has a very unpleasant odour.

If plants are left in their pots and plunged in moss or peat up to their rims, it is possible to mix all sorts of unlikely subjects together successfully for they can all be watered individually. Flowering plants can be happily included, and there will be complete flexibility. Plant pots can be changed around to alter the arrangement, so making the group planting much more interesting.

Mobile Displays

Another useful idea is to accommodate plants in a tray, again with an inch or so of gravel in the base, which is then in turn placed on a tea-trolley so that it can be placed near a window during the day and be taken to a warmer part of the room in the evening. It could even be placed under a wall or table lamp. Many plants benefit from this kind of treatment and the plants enhance the appearance of one another. The illustration opposite shows how such a tray might be used.

Plants on Pedestals

Having extolled the virtues of the fireplace as a plant area, it must now be mentioned that it is not the ideal place for plants when the room is full of people. The first few to enter will get the full enjoyment of the plants, but as the room fills up with people, the plants at ground level become ever less effective. The Victorians with their splendid plant pedestals had the answer to this problem: they lifted them off the floor for all to see – and if you have a collection of plants (or even one plant that you are proud of), then they should be displayed to fullest advantage.

If plant arrangements on pedestals are seldom effective, this is because the wrong plants are often chosen for the purpose. For the right plants we have to look back to the Victorian era. Their favourite plants for this purpose were the aspidistra and the nephrolepis fern, and with full-grown, mature plants of either you could not possibly wish for better pedestal subjects. In this setting, plants of all kinds seem to do especially well in respect of growth, as they have plenty of air all around them. One of the more modern house plants that is also effective as a pedestal plant is the Spider Plant, *Chlorophytum comosum*; but only as a large, mature plant that is possibly growing in a small hanging basket. The long stalks with scores of plantlets on the

This tray, with an inch or so of gravel covering its base, on which to stand the plants, includes (*from top centre, clockwise*) *Neanthe bella* **(Parlour Palm)**, *cryptanthus* **(Earth Star)**, *Asplenium nidus* **(Bird's Nest Fern)**, *tradescantia* and *Dracaena godseffiana*.

end can be most appealing when seen flowing away from the parent plant. Although most frequently seen as an upright-growing plant, the grape ivy, *Rhoicissus rhomboidea,* is also most attractive as a trailing plant on a pedestal.

In fact there is a very wide range of plants to choose from for pedestal positions. Many plants which normally are supported by canes can have them removed so that they become trailers. These include scindapsuses, ivies, tradescantias, *Cissus antarctica* and *Philodendron scandens*.

33

Hanging Plants

A few years ago the American house plant scene underwent a radical change when it seemed that everyone became obsessed with hanging plants. They hung from every post and rafter, cluttered up window areas and seemed to almost take over complete homes. It was assumed that the British would not hesitate to indulge in their usual habit of following the example of their American cousins. The ropes, the macramé kits, the hooks for suspending the pots and the pots themselves were imported, and we waited for lift-off. But we are still waiting, and I think we shall go on waiting. Although there has been reasonable interest, it has in no way followed the American pattern.

Why not, is something of a mystery, as having hanging plants indoors would appear to be an excellent way of showing off plants to maximum effect. Perhaps our rooms, in the main, are smaller, and there is the problem that hanging plants are likely to be bumped into at every turn. There is also the problem of caring for them; it is a much messier business trying to water plants suspended in mid-air than those on windowsills, tables, and the like.

Should you have hanging plants in your home, may I offer a word of advice – do not suspend the plant pots too high above the floor. The reason for this is that when plants are at eye level or thereabouts, it will be much easier to check their need for water. Watering will also be a much simpler operation, although wherever possible it is best to take the pot to the sink where the plant can be given a good drink without fear of spoiling the carpet (a consideration that is, so often, an excuse for underwatering).

If you are considering buying hanging plants and planters avoid tiny pots in which it is possible to put only tiny plants. Certainly the smaller the pots and planters, the cheaper they will be to buy, but it will be almost impossible to maintain the plants as they will dry out almost as quickly as you water them. It is much better to go for plants of reasonable size with good quantities of soil around their roots which will, in consequence need less frequent watering.

There are many fine trailing plants which can be used indoors, foremost among them the fine orange-red-flowered columneas, and *Columnea banksii* in particular. This plant flowers in the early part of the year – usually February, March, April – and, if well cared for, it will provide a really dazzling display.

Another columnea of slightly different habit is sold under two names, *Columnea crassifolia* and *C*. Firecracker. This plant has a slightly more compact habit which might be thought to set off the blooms to greater advantage.

Yet another fine flowering plant of trailing habit is *Episcia dianthiflora* which has small white flowers and masses of green leaves. It is a very simple plant to propagate and grows profusely if it is kept in a reasonably light position and is given ample water and feeding. For cooler conditions, possibly one of the finest of all flowering plants for this purpose is *Campanula isophylla*; in particular, *C. isophylla alba* which bears a profusion of star-like, white flowers throughout the summer months. It requires good light, lots of water and lots of feeding in order to succeed.

Also, among the easier plants is a wide selection of tradescantias and allied plants. If their growths are pinched out to encourage the formation of a bushy habit, and if they are grown in good light, they can be quite spectacular grown in this way, baskets or pots being suitable containers.

Ivies are also suitable for growing in this way, but generally speaking, they are better in cooler rather than warmer conditions. Many of the green-foliaged plants that one normally sees climbing up stick or cane supports – *Philodendron scandens*, *Rhoicissus rhomboidea* and plants of that kind – also make excellent trailers if their sticks are removed and they are allowed to just grow naturally.

There are several plectranthuses that one can use as hanging plants. These are all very easy to grow in conditions that range from quite cool to very warm without them seeming to suffer in any way. One important requirement is to ensure that they are fed regularly once they have become established.

A Question of Size

I am often confronted by people who wish to make a major house plant purchase – something about 10ft. (3m.) tall – to become a splendid corner piece for a room, often as an alternative to a piece of furniture. I ask them if they really mean 10ft. (3m.) tall, and would it not be a good idea to go back and measure the ceiling height of the room. Frequently, it transpires that it is a conventional room for which the plant is required, i.e., one with a ceiling height of some 8ft. (2.5m.). I mention this because, when buying larger plants, it is advisable to consider the question of height carefully and to obtain plants that are some 3ft. (1m.) shorter than the measurement from floor to ceiling. This will give the plants a chance to grow, and postpone the need for surgery for a reasonable length of time.

The lady who wrote to me to say that her Rubber Plant was touching the ceiling and turning left was advised that she should cut it back, but there was every chance that it would not only lose its top but also some of its lower leaves in the process. Healthy plants which are growing well will, surprisingly, tolerate quite severe pruning and not suffer unduly. The Rubber Plant is best cut back in the winter when there is very much less sap in the stem. Decide on the height you want the plant to be and, with a sharp pair of secateurs, sever the stem about 1in. (2.5cm.) above a leaf. There will be an inevitable loss of sap, but this can be checked by covering the wound with dry peat. As it is winter the plant will not be getting very much water, and one should continue with a restricted watering programme until such time as new growth is seen developing in the axils of the leaves near the top of the plant. From this time onwards more water can be gradually given. Following such surgery the plant will cease to have a single upright stem; instead there will be a number of growing points at its head which will usually give the plant a pleasing appearance.

The Need For Prudence

As the interest in house plants increases, so more and more unusual plants are becoming available and many of them, quite frankly, have no hope of surviving under normal conditions indoors. They are greenhouse plants that need the humid atmosphere and even temperature that generally prevails within the confines of a greenhouse. In such surroundings adjustments can be made to the heating, shading and ventilation which make it possible to grow the majority of tender tropical plants. But if you try to alter the atmospheric conditions in the home you run into all sorts of trouble. Growing conditions in the home are a compromise – you do the best you can for your plants with the resources at your disposal.

Creating an Environment

One way of improving the lot of more delicate small plants is to create an environment within an environment, and this can be done by having a miniature greenhouse, as it were, in the home or by making use of a carboy, for example, if the restricting confines of such a container are acceptable. One can go to the expense of having a large propagating case with heating cables running through the sand or other base on which the plants are placed. Many of the smaller plants will do very well in a warm, draught-free container of this kind.

Alternatively, find someone who has given up their interest in tropical fish or perhaps purchase a disused fish tank at a knock-down price. With a glass cover put over the top it will be found that such a container makes an excellent miniature greenhouse in which the humid atmosphere needed by the plants can be maintained.

Small ferns are ideal plants for closed cases, also fittonias, *Ficus radicans*, saintpaulias and *Neanthe bella*. The insectivorous Venus's Fly Trap (*Dionaea muscipula*) is a plant which no one in their right mind should ever contemplate purchasing; but if you must have one, then it will do a little better if it has a warm glass case in which to grow.

Plants in growing cases can be left in their pots, but those that are put into carboys have got to be removed from their pots and actually planted in the 5in. (13cm.) or so of peaty compost mixture that should be placed in the bottom of the container. Before introducing the mixture it is advisable to clean the container thoroughly with tepid water, and to keep the potting mixture away from the sides when it is being filled. It is often suggested that gravel should first be placed in the bottom of the carboy to 'assist drainage', but the water isn't going anywhere, so how can it possibly assist drainage? Although gravel is not essential, it is wise to mix in a few handfuls of charcoal when preparing the potting mixture – it will help to keep the mixture fresh.

A fish tank, with glass-covered top, converted into a miniature greenhouse. Saintpaulias (African Violets) grow on either side of a *Fittonia verschaffeltii* with a *Neanthe bella* (Parlour Palm) in the background.

In a large carboy no more than five small, slow-growing plants will be needed – any more and the bottle will be filled with congested foliage in no time at all. Any plants that are obviously outgrowing their neighbours should be ruthlessly pruned back with a razor blade fixed to a 2ft. (60cm.) cane, and any rot that is noted within the bottle, on plants or soil, should be cleared up immediately.

What you must do when selecting plants for carboys is to make sure that they are compact plants that are not likely to become too large too quickly. Far and away the best plants for this purpose are the small bromeliads such as cryptanthus and tillandsias as these are attractive in shape and they also remain compact without ever becoming invasive. The smaller peperomias are also suitable, these including *Peperomia caperata*, *P. hederaefolia* and *P. magnoliaefolia*. There are other peperomias that one might be tempted to include as they have nice small leaves, such as *P. resaediflora* but one would hesitate to recommend this rather rampant-growing plant. Many become especially vigorous once they are within the pleasant confines of a draught-free carboy.

Numerous very small ferns are also eminently suited to growing in bottle gardens, but one must be very careful not to choose small plants that are clearly going to grow into enormous subjects, and I'm thinking particularly of the nephrolepis ferns. Some of the forms of *Begonia rex* with smaller leaves would also be suitable in a larger carboy, but there is the difficulty of being able to treat them once they have been attacked by fungus diseases such as botrytis and mildew.

Flowering plants are seldom suitable as it is difficult to remove the flowers once they have died and begun to drop off. However, if you are able to get your hand into the container then there is no reason at all why smaller flowering plants such as saintpaulias should not be used. To give such a planting a touch of distinction, possibly the best plant to use is the miniature palm, *Neanthe bella*, and it will not become too large.

Sympathetic Lighting

Having got the right plant in the right place, one can considerably enhance its appearance by lighting it effectively. A painting can add tremendously to the appearance of a room and to accentuate its beauty it seems only natural to provide tasteful lighting to set it off. Plants, in their own way, serve the same purpose – they add something to the room. They also benefit from sympathetic lighting. There are now special lights available which have been developed specifically to improve the appearance and the performance of indoor plants. Strategically placed spotlights can also be used to very good purpose; but it is essential that such lights, which produce a considerable amount of heat, should not be too close to the plant, or plants. I have seen tough old palms and plants with similar leaves turn a rich shade of brown through having lights placed about 3ft. (1m.) away from them.

I am a great believer in using light to improve the growth of plants as well as to improve their appearance, but again there is a need for care in their positioning. Flowering plants such as saintpaulias can be improved out of all recognition just by placing the plants under a table lamp – there is no need to fit expensive spotlights.

Let me carry this aspect of plant care a little further. Plants die indoors for a number of reasons, and one of the major reasons is that plants are located in positions that do not offer them sufficient light in order to perform their natural growth functions. In order to succeed, house plants must have at least 700 to 800 lux*, although some of the tougher green-leaved philodendrons will survive, but not necessarily do well, at lower light levels. In the case of flowering plants, it would be very optimistic to expect them to produce flowers at light levels of less than one thousand lux – and this is a main reason why, to go back to African Violets again, so many people find it difficult to get apparently healthy plants to produce flowers for a second time in the home. Although many of the foliage plants will struggle through for a considerable time in poor light, it is absolutely essential for flowering plants to have the minimum amount mentioned.

A good example of the effect that light can have on the flowering performance of plants was the casual study I made recently of a 3ft. (1m.) diameter container filled with plants of *Hibiscus rosa-sinensis*, which was placed in a west-facing, almost full-light window. The plants in about one-third of the container nearest the glass flowered with reasonable freedom throughout the summer months, while those plants furthest

* Lux is a measurement of light difficult to define in layman's terms. However, the following guidelines may be helpful. A bright, sunny day is the equivalent of 80,000 lux; an overcast day, the equivalent of 5,000 lux. With cricket, bad light stops play at an average of 1,000 lux. Interior lighting in a modern office block gives an equivalent of 500 lux away from window areas.

away from the light source were extremely shy of flowering. Scorching of leaves may occur if plants are placed too close to window panes that are subjected to full, direct sunlight, therefore some protection will be needed during the hottest part of the day.

Providing plants with additional light by placing them close to an artificial light source during the evening will be of considerable benefit both in assisting plants to grow and encouraging flowering kinds to produce flowers more freely. There are a bewildering number of lights and combinations of lights that one may choose from, and it would be impossible to go into details about these here. Specialised lights to encourage plant growth are accredited with many and varied advantages, but my investigations and general experience suggest that there is not a great deal to choose between them, and that, at the end of the day, the house plant grower could well find that conventional, warm white fluorescent tubes will be as good a choice as any. However, there are variations and one can select specialised tubes that will enhance the appearance of the plants, though it will not necessarily improve their performance in respect of growth. When purchasing lights especially for growing plants, one should consult the supplier and ascertain the wattage required in order to obtain the minimum lux level that is recommended.

The further the light source is away from the plant then the less efficient it becomes. For example, a strip light fitted to the ceiling with the plants at floor level would not be anything like as efficient as the same light source brought nearer to the plants. However, it must be stressed that lights should not be too close to the plants and strip lights, for example, should not be closer than 2ft. (60cm.). In the case of spotlights, which generate much more heat, the distance between plant and light source would have to be considerably increased. Spotlights are an excellent method of highlighting particular plants.

In areas that are totally reliant on artificial light to encourage plant growth, it will be necessary to leave lights on for between 12 and 16 hours each day. For the benefit of the plants and for economic reasons it will be necessary to ensure that the plants are not exposed to continual artificial light during the night.

In poor light, plants with leaves which are completely green will do very much better than those with variegated foliage, and all plants growing in locations offering inadequate lux levels will become thin and etiolated.

Seasonal Pruning

At the end of the growing season – usually October–November – there will also be a need to trim back or prune some of the more untidy plants. In this respect, *Beloperone guttata*, the Shrimp Plant, immediately comes to mind, for it can be cut back quite severely with no great harm being done. But, generally speaking, it is better to tidy the plant up so that it has a more attractive shape and to leave it at that. In fact, the pieces that are removed will frequently make excellent cuttings from which new plants can be produced. Another plant that can be trimmed back at the end of its growing season is the hibiscus. Some hibiscuses grow to a considerable height and push out branches in all directions. It is worthwhile trimming them back to a more attractive shape during the later months of the year so that when new growth is produced in the spring, you have a compact, attractive and free-flowering plant.

Summer Airing

A change of air is frequently advocated as being beneficial to indoor plants. By that I mean placing the plants out of doors in the garden so that they can have a complete change of condition. This is all very well for the more tolerant plants during the summer months of the year, but I would hesitate to suggest that you should subject your codiaeums (Crotons), *Begonia rex*, or caladiums to this kind of treatment. But the ones that may be put outside – and these include even Rubber Plants (*Ficus elastica robusta*), sansevierias, and hibiscuses – should go into a sheltered corner where they will get a reasonable amount of sunlight but will not be affected by the blistering sun during the middle of the day. A lot of people – including many professionals – seem to think that if you place your plants out of doors where they are exposed to the rain, then there is no further need to water the pot. I don't agree, for the majority of house plants have reasonably large leaves and any water falling onto these is shed outside the pot rather than running into it. I would recommend that any plants placed out of doors should have their water requirements checked fairly regularly.

Now for plants which I would recommend for specific positions in the home:

Plants for the Hall

The hallway of the house is generally much cooler and subject to more draughts and other unpleasantnesses than the rest of the house. So for this area you will need plants that are more

Plants in a hall setting. *Left to right: Ficus elastica robusta* **(India Rubber Plant),** *Cissus antarctica* **(Kangaroo Vine)** and *Chlorophytum comosum* **(Spider Plant).**

tolerant of such conditions, and I would suggest that *Ficus elastica robusta*, the most popular Rubber Plant, is ideal for this situation (it likes to grow in reasonably good light and does not object to cooler conditions, provided the compost in which it is growing is not over-watered). Another suggestion is *Cissus antarctica*, which also does best in slightly cooler conditions, provided the temperature does not drop below 13°C. (55°F.). Its large, plain green leaves are quite attractive and it will climb readily if given adequate support.

Chlorophytum comosum is possibly the easiest of all the variegated plants we grow and is attractive with its grass-like appearance. The green and cream leaves produce small plantlets on the ends of long, arched stalks that add to the interest. Once it becomes a large plant, it is ideal, as I've already suggested elsewhere, for placing on a pedestal so that the young plantlets can be seen to best effect. Keep it fairly moist and feed it frequently and it must be repotted at least once a year if it is to retain its clean-cut appearance.

Plants for the Sitting-Room

The sitting-room is possibly the best place in the home in which to grow plants, for it usually provides good light and reasonable warmth, and someone is normally around to see to their needs. For this room the dracaenas are excellent, including *Dracaena godseffiana*, *D. deremensis* and *D. terminalis*. All require fairly good light and reasonably moist conditions and will have to be fed regularly during the spring and summer months. Also, in this room, under the same conditions, one can grow many of the fine flowering plants that are available, a special favourite of mine being *Begonia* Fireglow. With this plant you will also have to keep a careful watch for mildew on the leaves.

I would suggest also the aphelandra, the various forms of which will do well in lightly shaded conditions, provided the compost is kept moist all the time and the plants are reasonably well fed.

The same applies to *Beloperone guttata*, the Shrimp Plant, which does well on a light windowsill and can be pruned back to shape at the end of its growing season, which is normally October–November. Also, many primulas are available which will do extremely well on a light windowsill in a sitting room.

Another important flowering plant for this room is the Poinsettia, although it will do well in most rooms that are heated to a reasonable temperature. In the sitting-room it is almost sure to get exposure to good light conditions and reasonable warmth, and you will be able to enjoy the pleasure of its colourful red bracts for many months of the year. In addition to the plants mentioned, a very wide range of foliage plants would do well in this part of the house (see illustration for examples).

Plants in a sitting room setting. *Left to right: Cissus antarctica* (**Kangaroo Vine**), *Beloperone guttata* (**Shrimp Plant**), *Sansevieria trifasciata laurentii* (**Mother-in-Law's Tongue**), *Zebrina pendula* (**Wandering Jew**), *Dracaena deremensis, Philodendron scandens, Dracaena terminalis* **and tradescantia.**

Plants for the Dining-Room

The dining-room provides fairly good conditions for plants. It is generally smaller than the sitting-room, but the conditions prevailing are very similar, so again, we can choose from a wide range of foliage and flowering plants but perhaps the emphasis should be on foliage. The Grape Ivy, *Rhoicissus rhomboidea*, is perhaps the finest and most tolerant of all the green plants that we grow, and can be used as a climbing plant if it is provided with a framework on which to grow; it also makes an excellent pedestal plant with its foliage being most advantageously displayed when the growth can trail naturally. Sansevieria, Mother-in-Law's Tongue, is now available in forms other than the normal one, *Sansevieria trifasciata laurentii*, and all will do well in a light – a very light – position. They should not be

Plants in a dining room setting. *Left to right: Heptapleurum arboricola* (**Parasol Plant**), *Aechmea rhodocyanea* (**Urn Plant**), *Sansevieria trifasciata laurentii* (**Mother-in-Law's Tongue**), *Dracaena* **Red Edge,** *Vriesia splendens* and *Monstera deliciosa* (**Swiss Cheese Plant**).

given too much water and they will need very little, if any, feeding. They are perhaps the most tolerant of all house plants.

If there is space in the dining-room for its spreading growths and large leaves, the monstera or Swiss Cheese Plant is a good choice. It will require a support to which the branches can be attached or a mossed stake into which the aerial roots can root

46

naturally. In schefflera we have another very fine plant of architectural appearance and with spreading finger-like leaves that will attain a height of some 8 to 10ft. (2.5 to 3m.) in time, but this should not deter you, as it will take many years to reach such dimensions in average room conditions. The plant will need reasonable space in which to grow and, when watering, do this thoroughly and allow the plant to dry out a little before watering again. Feeding should not be neglected.

Schefflera is also subject to attack by red spider mite and the appropriate action should be taken as soon as their presence is realised.

Very similar in appearances to the schefflera but with much smaller leaves and a much more compact habit is the hepta-pleurum, of which three are now available, namely, *H. arboricola*, Geisha Girl (with more rounded leaves) and Hong Kong, which is a generally smaller and more compact plant. All have compound green-fingered leaves and one of their great attractions is that when the growing tip is removed, branching will occur at a lower level, so providing a much more compact and, I think, much more attractive plant. However, not everyone has a space for such things as monsteras and scheffleras in their dining-room, and one must then consider the smaller subjects. Perhaps the finest of these are the peperomias – in particular, *Peperomia hederaefolia* and *P. caperata*. These are ideal for small shelf areas and window ledges, bearing in mind that they will need reasonably good light but protection from full sunlight. In addition, the compost around their roots should never be too wet for too long.

Almost any of the bromeliads can be used in this part of the house, like *Vriesea splendens* and *Aechmea rhodocyanea*, as well as dracaenas, like *D. terminalis* and *D*. Rededge.

The codiaeum or Croton, also known as Joseph's Coat, is possibly the most colourful of all foliage plants grown in the house, and in order to retain its bright and colourful appearance, it should be placed on the lightest possible window ledge where it will get as much sunlight as possible. Crotons also need ample moisture at their roots, ample feeding and, when grown in pots rather than containers as shown in the illustration, potting on about once a year. Loss of leaves can usually be traced to inadequate heat (a temperature of about 20°C. [68°F.] is what is needed), insufficient water, or the fact that the plant has been placed in a shady corner. Indeed, a combination of all these ills would be fatal for almost all the Crotons you are likely to introduce into your home.

Plants for the Kitchen

The kitchen, like the dining-room, is an especially good place in which to grow house plants. Cyclamen do particularly well there because of the good light conditions generally available.

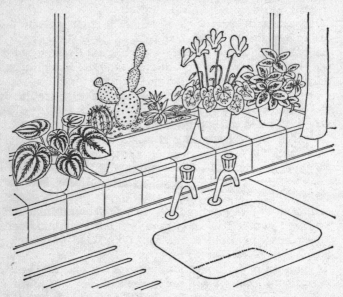

Plants in a kitchen setting. *Left to right: Peperomia sandersii,* **cacti, Florists' cyclamen and** *Perperomia magnoliaefolia.*

Many of the smaller-leaved peperomias like *Peperomia sandersii* and *P. magnoliaefolia* also do well there, and cacti, which are happy because there is usually less curtaining to cut down the available light.

Spring flowering plants will also do well here, for example, cinerarias, primulas and so on.

Plants for the Bedroom

The bedroom is possibly one of the most difficult rooms in the house in which to grow plants because the temperature is rarely steady for any length of time. One would hesitate to suggest filling the bedroom with plants and my feeling is that the single specimen plant is much more effective than a clutter of plants. One suggestion would be *Dracaena marginata*. Its gently arched leaves are narrow and pointed, striped cream and green with pinkish-red margins. It makes an excellent specimen plant.

The dear old aspidistra that will put up with any sort of treatment provided that it doesn't get too cold, is another good choice, as is *Ficus benjamina* (the weeping fig), although it can be a troublesome plant if grown in conditions which are too dark or if it is continually being moved from one part of the room to another.

Plant in a bedroom setting: *Kentia fosteriana* **(Kentia palm).**

Another plant suitable for the bedroom is the kentia palm *Kentia fosteriana* (see illustration). This can be bought as a mature plant or as quite a tiny one, when you can enjoy seeing it mature.

Plants for the Bathroom

The bathroom is an ideal place for plants. Generally speaking, it is most suitable for plants liking shade and moisture, and the philodendron in its many forms is an excellent choice. *Philo-*

Plants in a bathroom setting. *Philodendron scandens (left)* **and tradescantia.**

dendron scandens is a good plant for the small bathroom (it has small heart-shaped leaves), while *P. hastatum* is suitable if you have a bathroom reminiscent of Euston Station. This last can grow to a height of maybe 18 to 20ft. (5.5 to 6m.) and has broadly arrow-shaped leaves that are a pleasant shade of green. Ferns are also a good choice for the smaller bathroom, liking shade, moist conditions and reasonable warmth. Tradescantia also likes the moist conditions found in the bathroom.

CHAPTER FIVE

Perfect for Presents

Two things which are guaranteed to make me feel off-colour for weeks are the thought of going out to buy Christmas presents and choosing new wallpaper. There are always so many reasons why you should not get whatever it is you are looking at. And, in the case of presents, there is always the possibility that the recipient will already have what you choose, and may not want it anyway.

But with plants you are safe – virtually everybody likes them as presents. Good plant shops always have a wide selection at varying prices, but it has to be said that there are also many shops which cater only for those wanting lower-priced plants – for the very good reasons, usually, that they cannot provide suitable conditions for more exotic plants or the knowledgeable staff to look after them. So, seek out one of the first kind if you can.

Believe it or not, if a plant succumbs soon after it has been handed over as a gift it seems to reflect on the bestower. So, when buying plants as presents, do it with some care! I give suggestions for plant presents during the four seasons of the year on pp. 55 to 60.

I get many letters from people who have received house plants as gifts, and they are clearly suffering as much distress as the plants which are wilting, shedding their leaves and in various other stages of disability. You can feel it in their letters – some mention the agonising predicament, 'What am I going to do when my friend calls and sees what I have done to the plant?' The fault may not lie with either the donor or the recipient, as the plant might well have been an inferior one in the first place and doomed to die whatever the care given it after it arrived. So, when buying plants, make sure that both foliage and flowering kinds have a fresh, clean look about them. The considerate supplier will ensure that even the pot in which the plant is growing has been wiped clean to give the plant a better overall appearance.

Almost all plants look better when their pots are put into outer containers (or covers), many of which are inexpensive to buy. Avoid those with garish patterns. No doubt the intention of the manufacturer is to make the container more colourful and eye-catching than the plant it is intended to complement. This is quite wrong. The object of the pot cover is to enhance the overall appearance of the plant, not compete with it.

But you can never tell with people – it sometimes seems that when it comes to colour, anything goes. In a wild moment I purchased a small quantity of pot covers with a velvet texture (flock) finish, most of them in breathtaking colours. Having lamented the fact that we should all have to start wearing sunglasses, and that no one in their right mind would dream of buying them, almost the first customer of the day married up one of brightest blue with a very bright red *Dracaena terminalis*. An unhappier combination you could not imagine. Perhaps it was for her mother-in-law!

I am very conservative in my ways and when it comes to selecting pot covers I feel that they should be of clean design, and that there are only two colours (if you discount the natural terra-cotta of clay pots) that go well with plants, and they are white and dark brown.

I have mentioned elsewhere the necessity for inspecting wrapped plants before actually buying them. It is also important in cold weather to make sure that the plant is properly protected before taking it outdoors. It offends me to see tender plants being carried along the street in cold weather with the top of the plants exposed to the air. After all, it is the plant that matters, and codiaeums (Crotons), dieffenbachias and dracaenas that have no protection for their more tender top leaves may well succumb before you get them home. So have your new plant wrapped well and carefully.

Planted Bowls

Having exhausted all the possibilities in the way of individual plants, you may well feel that Granny would be happy with a planted bowl – a collection of plants in the same container. There are hidden dangers here. Something that must be avoided is the very small bowl completely congested with plants, as it is a sign that the bowl has been hastily put together and the plants have little chance of survival. Plants in bowls must have reasonable space in which to develop or they will simply rot and die.

It is wise also to check the height of the plants in relation to the depth of the container in which they are planted. The reason for this is that you frequently see plants up to 2ft. (60cm.) tall in containers that are little more than 3in. (8cm.) deep. You would have to be a genius to grow plants of that size in a container of that depth. Invariably, such plants are grown in pots of 5in. (13cm.) diameter and with a depth of about 6in. (15cm.) and to get it into the shallower container the roots must be mutilated. The plant may well survive, and it could even do very well, but there is a much more likely prospect of it objecting to such treatment once it has been introduced to the harsher conditions (for plants) of the average living-room. So what I am really saying is that you might be wiser not to be lured into purchasing the largest and most luxuriant of the planted bowls that may be on offer.

My postbag suggests that many owners of planted bowls wonder what they should do when the plants in them get out of hand – the Grape Ivy, *Rhoicissus rhomboidea*, in particular seems to be prone to exceptionally vigorous growth and to overshadow all the other occupants of the bowl.

The answer is to remove such offenders from the mixed container and plant them individually in pots of at least 5in. (13cm.) in diameter, using a reasonably peaty house-plant potting compost mixture. Smaller fry can be re-planted in the bowl where they can be expected to be happy, freed from the overpowering presence of their more vigorous former neighbours.

Suiting the Plant to the Person

When buying plants as gifts, it is very important that you should choose plants which will be reasonably compatible with their new home. If Granny has a room that is a bit old-fashioned, a bit dark and not very warm, then she ought to be given a tough sort of plant. Something from the easier range of house plants will be the most appropriate (and most plants have labels attached to them indicating whether they are easy or difficult to grow). Although it may be less exciting to look at, such a plant will present the old lady with far fewer problems and that can be a blessing in itself.

The Easy Way of Growing

In complete contrast to Granny, the newlyweds may prefer something that is swinging and 'with it' – even if they know as much about house plant care as they know about pot-holing. I feel it might be best in such circumstances to consider the most recent innovation in house plant cultivation to go with fashionable furniture and furnishings – a plant grown by the Hydroculture method, i.e., one that has its own water supply built in, as it were. (For a description of this method, see pp. 185 to 190.) Such plants need not complicate the lives of the new home makers as the cultural attention they need amounts to little more than re-filling the water reservoir about once every three weeks and re-charging the unit with fertiliser every six or 12 months, depending on the type of container that the plant is growing in.

Hydroculture-grown plants can be bought in a number of different containers, including large ones which can be filled with a selection of plants that would not look out of place in a mansion. This kind of plant display can also be ideal in office surroundings.

Seasonal Possibilities

One of the principal reasons why 'plants are perfect for presents' is that almost every plant is different, and even if you buy a cyclamen for someone who already has one, there is very little chance that the plants will be identical. A selection of plants for each of the four seasons of the year follows. Some of the seasons of display will inevitably overlap, but the ones that are listed should be available at the particular time mentioned. I would repeat that, when choosing presents, it is very important to think in terms of the conditions that the plant is likely to be subjected to and buy one which is appropriate. Choose wisely.

Spring Choices

For spring, let's start with the various forms of *Hydrangea macrophylla* which are available in many different colours from white, through pinks, to very attractive shades of blue. These need a fairly light position indoors and fairly cool conditions, and they must be adequately watered. One of their principal attractions is the fact that when they have done their duty indoors they can be planted out in the garden to grow on and serve as a permanent reminder to the recipient of the person who made the gift.

Next, I would suggest one of the forms of *Azalea indica*. This is rather an expensive plant, but it is also very eye-catching and not at all difficult to manage if it can be given cool conditions and abundant water at its roots at all times. When it has finished flowering, remove the dead blooms and, when there is no longer any chance of a frost occurring, place it out in the garden, preferably in a shaded location, where it can remain until the end of September, when it should be brought indoors again. During its time out of doors, water it abundantly and spray its foliage periodically.

Another flowering plant for this time of year is the very inexpensive Busy Lizzie or impatiens, which is available in many colours and not at all difficult to manage provided it has good light, plenty of water and plenty of food. It is a good idea to suggest to the person to whom you are giving the plant that it should be repotted straight away into a slightly larger container. A good foliage plant to give as a present at this time of the year (or at any time of the year if it comes to that) is *Monstera deliciosa*, for it has a very distinctive appearance and is able to withstand all sorts of conditions indoors without coming to too much harm. And finally, a great favourite of mine, *Hedera canariensis variegata*, the Canary Island Ivy, which has green and cream variegated leaves, grows very well as an upright plant and, when it has lost its attraction as an indoor plant, can be planted out of doors to make an excellent climber to clothe a wall or fence.

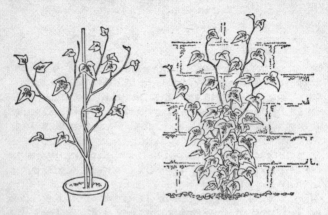

When the variagated Canary Island Ivy, *Hedera canariensis variegata*, has become jaded as a house plant, move it into the garden and give it a new lease of life.

Summer Choices

The summer is a good time to buy plants that are just a little bit more temperamental, for they then have a chance to settle down in the more agreeable conditions that prevail at that time. The first plant on my list would be *Heptapleurum arboricola* with its elegant green foliage and ability to withstand difficult conditions without too much bother. Another foliage plant would be the codiaeum (Croton) which is an excellent plant for indoors in summer as it then has the chance to get well established before winter arrives. Codiaeums need good light, plenty of water and plenty of feeding.

As to flowering plants for summer, possibly the most important introduction of recent years is *Begonia* Fireglow. Fireglow is a little misleading as a name, for it comes, as I've explained elsewhere (see p. 21), in all sorts of other colours besides red –

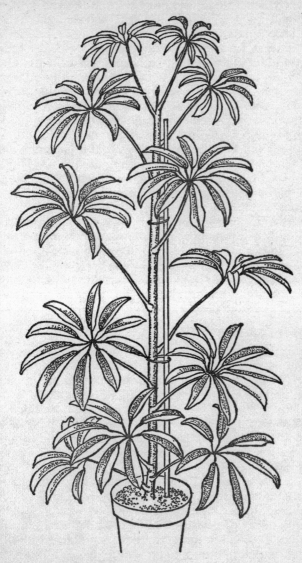

Heptapleurum arboricola (**Parasol Plant**).

whites, yellows, creams and many more. It is a very tolerant plant and does particularly well in light conditions and reasonable temperatures. It should be kept moist and an eye should be kept open for mildew on the leaves and stems, this being treated with Benlate fungicide as soon as it is noticed.

Next in flowering plants is the pelargonium (Geranium) which again is available in many colours and is not at all difficult to manage, but it will need plenty of feeding and watering to keep it in good condition. If the plant you buy looks too large for its pot, then move it straight away into a slightly larger one and it will be sure to flourish. It is important with pelargoniums to watch for white fly on the undersides of leaves and to combat this immediately with the appropriate insecticide.

Finally, one of my great favourites among flowering plants – the saintpaulia. The saintpaulias are also available in many colours and with single or double flowers, while some even have interesting patterns on their leaves. All of them need good light in which to grow, and this will mean placing them on a light windowsill which is not exposed to too much direct sunshine. They can then be put under a wall light or table lamp in the evening. When watering use tepid water and try to keep it off the leaves at all costs.

Autumn Choices

During the autumn months and in the weeks before Christmas, one of the most appropriate gifts, I feel, is a planted arrangement, where several different varieties of plants are grouped together in the same container. These arrangements make excellent gifts as they are rather dramatic and colourful. The most important thing to be aware of with these, however, is that most of these bowls have no drainage holes at the bottom, so watering must be done carefully, and never to excess (see page 64).

A new plant that will certainly be interesting to the person who owns a collection of plants already is *Ficus* Europa, a variegated Rubber Plant that has withstood many tests and is proving to be a particularly suitable subject for indoor culture.

When seeking something expensive for a very particular friend or relation, there is *Citrus mitis* to consider. This is the

Calamondin Orange which is of dwarf habit and produces an abundance of tiny oranges. These are edible but I find that they are better when used for making marmalade. My own plant seems to enjoy life out of doors more than it enjoys life indoors, but provided it is kept well watered it is not a problem.

Another interesting possibility is the hanging planter, that is to say, a macramé hanger with an attractive pottery container into which the plant is either planted or merely set. There are any number of plants which can be used for this purpose, but possibly one of the most colourful and certainly one of the easiest to grow is the tradescantia. Tradescantias are available with silver, gold and many other colourings and always have a fascination for the indoor plantsman.

When purchasing presents, there is always the person who has everything, and this applies with plants as well as other items in the house. So you have to look for something different that is going to cause a bit of a stir. Here I would suggest you might well look for one of the larger-leaved philodendrons, and in particular, *Philodendron hastatum* which has large, roughly arrow-shaped, broad green leaves. It grows into a majestic specimen. But this, I must emphasise, is not for the tiny living-room where there is little room to turn round.

Winter Choices

In winter, as we approach Christmas, the choice is much wider, both in terms of foliage and flowering plants, so it may seem a little odd that I should suggest the possibility of buying a small collection of cacti. Many people find a collection of this kind quite fascinating. Cacti can be reasonably priced and a small group on a windowsill can be very effective. They are very easy to look after, the principal need being that they should be well-watered between spring and early autumn, and from autumn through until early spring be given no water whatsoever. They need a light position and reasonable warmth – other than that, they are very little bother.

Similar in many ways to the cacti is the sansevieria. There are several forms available and they are extremely tolerant plants that will grow in almost any conditions provided that they are not too wet or too cold. But they are not everyone's choice, so it may be as well to find out beforehand whether or not your friends approve of cacti and sansevierias.

Another possibility at this time of year is a plant grown by the Hydroculture method. Many plants are offered in this way nowadays and they are very easy to look after, doing exceptionally well in the hands of beginners (see p. 185).

Then there is the cyclamen which, although it presents many problems for many people, is still one of the most popular of all flowering plants. It needs good light and cool conditions and should be well-watered and allowed to dry out before watering again. In my experience the kitchen windowsill is by far the best place for them indoors.

Last of all the Poinsettia, which a few years ago was looked upon with some trepidation as a difficult plant. Now it is one of the easiest of flowering plants available in winter. And the reason for that is the work of the plant breeders who have improved it tremendously. We now have really superb plants that grow to only 18 to 20in. (45 to 50cm.) tall and can be controlled at that height by using growth-retardants. They are available with bracts of red, pink or white. In fact, it is not unusual to find Poinsettias bought in December still bearing their coloured bracts (the flowers in the centre of the bracts are small and insignificant) in the following August and September – and if that is not good value, nothing is!

CHAPTER SIX

Stop, You're Killing Me!

Following a radio programme during which there had been much discussion about talking to plants, Dusty, the studio engineer, said, 'The next thing you'll know, the plants will be answering back!' I thought that such a possibility could have its advantages – the plants could make known their needs for less feeding, less water, more warmth, cooler conditions, more light or less sunshine, and with the occasional one saying, perhaps, 'Could something be done about the greenfly feeding off my top leaf?'

Nice to think of as a possibility, but the reality is that we have to rely on our instincts and what we see with our eyes to interpret the needs of plants. Alternatively (and this is what 'green fingers' may, in part, be about), we can anticipate the requirements of our plants, and see the signs of impending danger before disaster strikes. Noting, for example, the first signs of dark, sooty mould on the upper surfaces of leaves should cause one immediately to inspect the undersides of the leaves directly above. As often as not the inspection will result in the discovery of scale insects clinging like miniature limpets to the undersides of the leaves, and to the stems and leafstalks. Other pests may also be responsible, but scale usually leaves the messiest mould. The mould grows on the excreted deposits of the insects and does little harm to the plant, but for appearance's sake it should be wiped off with a damp sponge.

The ability to detect the presence of the minute red spider mite on plants is another skill that is worth acquiring, as this pest can be particularly damaging if left unchecked for any length of time. Red spider seems to have its favourite feeding plants but is not over-particular and is first noticed by a slight discolouration of the topmost young leaves of the plant. As the attack worsens, so the leaves become more discoloured, take on a much drier appearance and have a tendency to curl under at their margins. By very close observation one can detect red spider with the naked eye, but a magnifying glass will make them more easily discernable. The variegated ivy, *Hedera canariensis variegata* (syn. *H*. Gloire de Marengo), is a plant that is frequently affected, and mites are difficult to see on the white colouring of leaves. When well established, red spider will form minute webs on the undersides of leaves and in the area where the leaf is attached to the leafstalk. This troublesome pest appears to be at home in almost any conditions, but seems to thrive and multiply more freely where the atmosphere is very dry and warm.

These are only two of the many problems that may beset one's plants, but with experience one can detect and control many of the threats long before the plants have come to much harm. The ability to detect signs of poor growth, the presence of pests and so on will serve you best when making plant purchases. With a little experience you will soon know which plants to avoid.

If you have bought or been given a sick plant, it will have very little chance of surviving indoors, where growing conditions are often far from ideal. So, when buying plants, don't be too influenced by the 'Oh, it will be all right' attitude. Having bought a plant, make sure that it is properly wrapped if the weather is in any way inclement.

There is another thing to be aware of with newly-bought plants. Often these will have been grown in greenhouses shaded from direct sunshine, so, on getting them home, those which need light positions should be gradually conditioned to the stronger light. Place them out of direct sunshine.

Leaf-cleaning Chemicals

There is one time when no plant, however sun-tolerant it may be, should be placed in direct sunlight and that is when it has just had its leaves cleaned with one of the many chemical concoctions that are available for this purpose. Many plants are spray-cleaned with a white oil to enhance their appearance before leaving the nursery on which they have been raised. So, any plants which have an oily sheen to their leaves when you buy them should under no circumstances be placed in direct sunlight. It is also inadvisable to expose them to cold conditions. In normal, average temperatures, cleaning oils will do no harm and will improve the overall appearance of the plant, but do avoid subjecting plants so treated to extremes of temperature or light.

Having got the plant home there could be many reasons for it to cry out, 'Stop, you're killing me!' It will, in all probability, object to the fact that it has been removed from its pleasant greenhouse environment, been taken to a shop and then to a home. As we all know, homes vary considerably – some are light, airy and well heated (which will suit our plant fine); others are cold, dark and miserable, and not at all the sort of environment that a house plant finds congenial.

Optimum Conditions

Should the new plant be one of the many flowering kinds it will, in most cases, prefer a cool, light and airy room that is heated to a temperature in the region of 13° to 16°C. (55° to 60°F.). Exact temperatures are almost impossible to achieve in the average home, but remember that the majority of flowering plants will last longer and stay fresher in cool conditions. Hot, airless conditions are what they dislike. Cyclamen, for example, will quickly show signs of displeasure if given this kind of treatment, and yellowing of leaves will soon let you know that you are killing it if the room temperature is excessively high and the atmosphere very dry. If you find that your plant wilts from under-watering, place it in a bowl of water until the compost is thoroughly moistened; tie paper wrapping round it to secure the growths and provide protection, and leave until these are firm once again.

You can also kill house plants through kindness. For example, by feeding plants too soon after they have been potted into new soil – most plants are best left for about six months after potting on before feeding is re-started. They can also be fed too frequently, at a rate of application far in excess of that recommended by the manufacturer. But by the same token, almost any plant that you may acquire will need regular feeding to prosper. Some manufacturers of house plant liquid feeds recommend that a little of their product should be put in the water each time the plant is watered – but this would be a very small amount. Even so, it is probably better to feed in this fashion rather than give plants excessive amounts at infrequent intervals. Overfeeding damages the roots of the plants, and this damage is eventually made apparent when they begin to develop discoloured leaves.

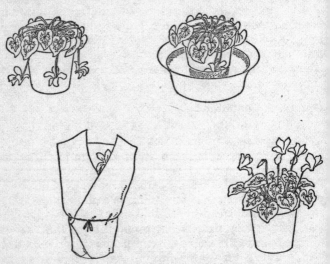

Reviving a wilting cyclamen by placing it in a bowl of water until the compost is thoroughly moistened, when wrapping paper is tied round the growths to give them support until they are firm once again.

Aspects of Watering

Almost more important than feeding is watering, and this is possibly the most difficult aspect of plant care to understand. It is not so much a question of knowing how much water the plant requires, it is more a question of knowing when to stop. During the summer months, plants will not object too strongly to occasional overwatering as they are growing more vigorously and will require more water anyway. During the winter months, overwatering becomes a much more acute problem as plant growth is less active and the growing conditions are often less agreeable, and you can all too easily end up with a plant looking like the *Ficus benjamina* illustrated here.

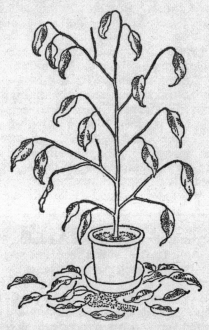

A sad example of an overwatered *Ficus benjamina* **(Weeping Fig).**

A good example of a generally very tolerant plant that quickly succumbs if kept too wet for too long is *Aralia sieboldii* (syn. *Fatsia japonica*). It is hardy out of doors and grows very well in a light and cool situation indoors if allowed to dry out a little between each watering; but if it remains wet for long periods the roots become damaged and the leaves droop alarmingly. When plants are first introduced to indoor conditions, be particularly careful with watering, certainly until the needs of the particular plant are better understood. I have long since given up the difficult task of giving precise directions about the amount of water this or that plant should have. The trouble is that some people do the oddest things to their plants and still get the most marvellous results. To illustrate this point there is the case of the visitor to one of the Royal Horticultural Society's Westminster shows some years ago to whom I talked about her Mother-in-Law's Tongue (sansevieria), which she had purchased from a local nurseryman. He had suggested that she should water her plant once each year in the month of August (when the plant was bought, as it happened). I thought to myself that the man must have been out of his mind to suggest such spartan treatment, even for the very tolerant sansevieria. But instead of voicing this opinion, I asked, 'How long did it last?' To my amazement she said she had had it for four years and it was a marvellous plant. You never can tell! I knew that the succulent leaves of the sansevieria had a capacity for storing a considerable amount of moisture, but one year's supply was much more than I would have reckoned.

The age-old practice of placing a knowledgeable thumb on top of the compost in the pot to decide whether it is dry or wet still continues. Many people find it difficult to believe that you can actually look at the plant and pot and decide whether it is wet or dry – in the latter condition, the leaves may be slightly limp, or the surface of the soil may have taken on a whitish-grey, as opposed to a dark brown, colouring. Another way to form an opinion is to lift the pot and note the weight – if it is very heavy in proportion to its size it is usually wet, and if it feels as if it is about to blow away it is obviously too dry.

Then there are those plants that need more water than others – the azalea, for example must be kept wet all the time, but it must not actually stand in water. One really golden rule is that the soil must never be so dry that it actually shrinks and leaves a gap between the soil and the side of the pot. Even for the tolerant sansevieria this sort of treatment could prove too much. One thing is certain – in time, if you have any ability at all, you get to know the needs of your plants.

The Holiday Problem

Such information can be most valuable when the time for the annual vacation draws near and you are wondering what to do with your plants. Well-meaning neighbours can be too attentive for the good of the plants and knowing their needs makes it possible to give them precise written instructions for individual plants which they can keep in their home while you are away. Don't completely denude the window-ledges, however, as this tells every passer by that the house is empty – the almost indestructible Mother-in-Law's Tongue can be left on guard and will come to no harm during your absence if the house is reasonably warm.

So, leaving the odd few plants to be looked after by a neighbour presents few problems provided the instructions are adequate. The enthusiast who is leaving a roomful of plants is in a different category. It is then much better to have a trusted friend to come in and administer to the needs of the plants. But a proper briefing is even more necessary in such cases. Naturally, the person most suited for this chore is someone who has a collection of plants of their own. My own house plants, patio planters and greenhouse, are carefully looked after by my nearest neighbours when I am on holiday, and I reciprocate by caring for their plants when they are away. This works so well that arrangements are made far in advance to ensure that we are not on holiday at the same time. Ensuring that plants are cared for at times like this is as important for many of us as caring for pets, and I never cease to be amazed at the lengths to which plant enthusiasts will go to make sure that their charges get the right attention.

If no one can be found to look after the plants, then it will be necessary to take alternative action. Rubber Plants, Swiss Cheese Plants, Spider Plants, cacti and numerous other tolerant plants will usually do perfectly well if they are well-watered just before you leave and placed out of direct sunlight. Some may even be the better for the rest from watering!

To help retain moisture one can place the plants in a large container filled with damp peat into which the plant pots can be plunged to their rims. Wet sphagnum moss, even wet newspaper, can also serve as a surround for plant pots to keep them moist for a longer period. Several inches of wet sand placed in a deep, watertight tray will also help to retain moisture and keep the plants happy during your absence – the plant pots should first be watered, then pressed gently into the sand so that water may be drawn up by capillary action. Decorative pot covers should, of course, be removed, and clay pots will need to have cotton wool or a felt wick pushed into the bottom of each pot in order to bridge the gap between compost and sand which you get with thicker-based pots such as these.

Surrounding your plants with moisture-retaining material could well prevent them being killed off at times other than the annual vacation. So many plants miss the moist conditions of the greenhouse which forms a better environment for them. This is a good substitute. You can soon kill plants, too, by placing them on ledges immediately over hot radiators, for this will dry out the foliage and tend to cause dehydration. Conversely, one may do a plant just as much harm by placing it in a position where it is to be exposed to constant cold draughts – fresh air entering a room from an open door or window on a warm day is a different matter, for that is essential to the well-being of plants.

Pest and Disease Control

What about insecticides and fungicides ? These are available in bewildering numbers and in very attractive packs that simply ask to be purchased. They are so simple to use (puffers, aerosols, dabbers, systemics – there is no shortage), and there seems to be a deterrent for any pest you care to mention. But still the pests come to plague us with uncanny persistence.

My view is that we tend to get carried away by the prospect of all these pesticides and fungicides, and that we use them much too frequently and too liberally. When one is talking about a few plants in the home, the most primitive means of destruction are still the best. Squashing pests is by far the most certain way of ensuring that they are truly dead – gentle squeezing between finger and thumb has a strangely fatal effect on greenfly in particular. But if squashing greenfly does not appeal, you could use the very old-fashioned remedy of soapy water – either spray it on to the leaves, or, if the plants are small, have a bucketful of the stuff and invert pot and plunge into the soapy water.

Another simple and inexpensive alternative for getting rid of many pests is to use a sponge or soft cloth and clean the beasties off the plant. Provided plant leaves are not very brittle or tender, I cannot see any reason why wiping the undersides of leaves with a moist sponge regularly should not eradicate the very persistent whitefly. You may not be able to kill all the flies as they dart about, but there should be no difficulty in wiping away the eggs and preventing them breeding. You can try all sorts of insecticides but there is no doubt in my mind that a sponge applied with a little pressure is far and away the best method of getting rid of scale insects on the odd few plants.

In the past few years there has been an abundance of ladybirds, and a handful of these collected from the garden and placed on pest-ridden plants can have a magical effect as they set about devouring a ready-made meal. The greenfly on my hibiscus plants simply vanish in moments, and when they have more or less licked the leaf clean, our plump and spotted ladybirds are transferred to the garden to continue their excellent work.

The mealy bug can provide problems, and squashing them by hand is not a pleasant exercise. Instead you may prefer to use the time-honoured piece of cotton wool tied to a slender cane and dipped in methylated spirits; this is still a simple and effective remedy. The cotton wool blob is soaked in methylated spirits and is then applied directly on to the bugs. The bugs themselves have the appearance of miniature wood-lice that have painfully made their way through a bowl of flour that has left them covered in a white powdery deposit. To kill them it is essential that the insecticide should make direct contact, but having killed the adults there is very little hope that the insecticide will have the slightest effect on the baby bugs that are wrapped and sealed in what, for all the world, appears to be a cocoon made of cotton wool. The methylated spirits will kill the bug when contact is made, but the cocoon will have to be completely removed by careful use of the cotton wool dabber.

Plants may also be attacked by root mealy bug, which is seen as a whitish powder around the roots of the plant with the bugs themselves going about their destructive business. These are also very persistent pests that can be eradicated by drenching the soil with diluted malathion or similar insecticide. But this treatment is not always successful, and malathion smells abominably. Rather drastic, but another cure that will cost nothing (if one's natural apprehension is ruled out!) is to invert the pot and hold a hand over the soil while the pot is tapped on the edge of a table or bench and the pot is removed leaving one with the exposed root ball. Always water the plant prior to

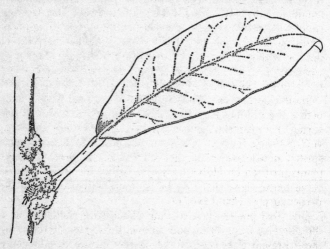

A mealy bug and its typical cotton-wool-like cocoon.

attempting this operation. You then remove all the soil from around the roots, before washing them gently in water so that all the soil and all the root mealy bug is removed. You can then carefully repot the plant into a slightly smaller pot, teasing the new soil around the roots as the pot is gradually filled up. Hold the plant erect and tap the pot repeatedly as the operation progresses – this will ensure that the soil settles around the roots. I know, I can hear you saying what a daft suggestion that is for some plants – and for plants that produce masses of fleshy and tightly compacted roots, such as monsteras and clivias, the chances of washing the roots free of soil would be almost nil. But there are a great many plants that can be treated in this way and the elimination of root mealy bug should not present too many difficulties. It is also difficult to treat large and unwieldy plants in this way – the only alternative is to thoroughly drench the soil with malathion or other suitable insecticide which is effective against this particular pest.

It is wise to treat all the insecticides and fungicides that one may use with complete respect, and to assume that they are all toxic and likely to present problems if they are negligently handled. This will mean locking them away, and wearing rubber gloves every time they are being mixed or applied. Treating plants indoors is inadvisable, and the best way of dealing with pests on plants that are in need of spraying or whatever, is to take them out of doors on a still, warm day and to apply the chemical in a shady place.

Indiscriminate use of such chemicals on all your plants before the product has been tested can also be a way of ensuring that plants will be emitting that silent cry of 'Stop, you're killing me!' It is very much better to test any new sprays, powders and the like on smaller replicas of larger plants, or even on individual leaves before the entire plant is subjected to those that may be far more lethal to it than the particular pest would ever be.

One final point, when treating plants with chemicals do a thorough job by covering both sides of the leaves and repeating the treatment after seven to 10 days to ensure that hatching young are also eliminated. But don't forget that hand-cleaning of plants may be much more positive in its results, and it will not be so expensive – there is the Scot coming out in me!

Repotting Pitfalls

The possibility of killing plants with kindness has already been mentioned, and this is seldom more evident than when it comes to repotting plants into larger containers. The considerate owner will ensure that the potting medium being used is something that has been properly prepared and not some soil from the garden. But often enough the same considerate person will have this terrible fetish for potting the plant on with ridiculous frequency. The result is that the plant is eventually in a container that is much too large for it and completely out of proportion to its size.

Ideally, the plant should look right, with the height and spread being balanced by the pot in which it is growing. It is not only aesthetically undesirable if the reverse is the case (as

A distinct case of over-potting! Plant and pot should have a balanced appearance.

in the illustration); it can be lethal for all but the most durable plants, as there is a marked tendency for the potting mixture in such conditions to turn sour long before the plant has been able to establish itself in the new medium. Most plants will go for one year without the need for potting on, and many will go for two or more years, provided they are correctly fed. Once plants have found their way into pots that are 10in. (25cm.) in diameter, there is generally little need to pot them on further, but feeding will again be essential. To require a pot any larger than this a plant would really have to be something of a monster.

Conversely, don't let the plants get so pot-bound that almost the whole pot area is taken up by a mass of congested roots, as in the illustration below.

People have odd ideas at times about pot size in relation to plant height – even intelligent people. An architect came to me one day to say he needed a plant of character some 3.75m. (12ft.) tall to go into a disused lift-shaft which had glass sides and could be viewed from all round. From a distance he showed obvious enthusiasm for a splendid specimen of that fine plant, *Ficus lyrata*, the Fiddle-leaf Fig. On coming abreast of the plant and seeing the pot in which it was growing his earlier enthusiasm melted and his face took on a somewhat pained

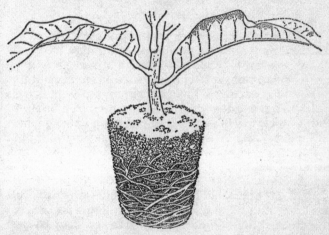

An example of a plant long overdue for repotting, as indicated by the matted root system.

expression. After a deep swallow he rather sheepishly told me that only the previous day he had had two men dig a hole in the bottom of the lift-shaft some 3ft. (1m.) deep and the same in diameter. The hole was to accommodate the very large pot the architect thought the plant would be growing in – and the reason for his embarrassment was that the hole had been dug out of solid concrete! The ficus was very comfortably nestled in a pot no more than 12in. (30cm.) in diameter and of similar depth.

73

CHAPTER SEVEN

Raising Plants and Keeping Them Happy

There is no greater pleasure than raising one's own plants, whether this is from seed, cuttings, or by other means. By doing this you also get additional plants at comparatively small cost – but don't expect all of these started on the windowsill to be as good as those cared for initially by the professional in his carefully controlled greenhouse environment. But have a go and you could well be surprised by your green-fingered ability.

The first thing to understand when venturing into plant propagation is not to be too ambitious at the outset. Start with the easy things and get the feel of it before demonstrating to everyone what a clever house-plant grower you are! I have stressed this before, but it is so much more satisfying to root and grow on an Ivy or a pilea successfully than it is to attempt to increase Crotons, for example, and then have to watch them deteriorate and die off.

Raising Plants From Seed

The cheapest and most simple way of starting a collection of plants is to grow them from seed. It will also provide you with surplus plants which you can exchange or simply pass on to interested friends. The easiest plant to start with could well be the coleus, the foliage plant that comes in almost every colour imaginable.

First purchase your packet of seed and read the instructions on the reverse of the packet, which will tell you the time to sow, whether the seed should be covered or left on the surface, the eventual height of the plant and so on. Cleanliness is a prime factor when it comes to successful propagation, so a few handfuls of soil from the garden will not normally be good enough. I favour a mixture of fresh sphagnum peat with just enough sand added to make it possible to feel it between the fingers when a little of the mixture is rubbed together. Sharp sand should be used and not the normal smooth builder's sand, but you will only need about three handsful to mix with enough peat to fill the average-sized seed box. If preferred, the John Innes seed compost can be used, but it is important that it should be fresh and not a dry and lifeless mixture that has been lying around waiting for a customer for the previous 12 months.

Whatever growing medium is used, it should be watered and mixed with the hands to ensure that it is thoroughly wetted – and that doesn't always happen when the watering is done with a can after the mixture has been put in the box. So, this compost must be moist but not totally saturated. After sowing, cover the seed with a thin dressing of sand and then water with a can that has a fine rose attached. Place the box in a temperature of not less than 16°C. (60°F.) and out of direct sunlight. Cover the box with a sheet of glass and cover this in turn with a sheet of newspaper. These are left in position until the seed has germinated. During the germinating period the glass should be periodically removed and any condensation that has formed wiped away before it is replaced.

Once germination has taken place, the seedlings will need good light but protection from the sun and, presuming they are coleus seedlings, they can be transferred when large enough to handle into small pots. Water the compost and handle the young plants by the leaves with great care; never hold them by the tender young stems. A pointed stick can be used to tease the roots of adjacent seedlings apart so that the minimum damage is done to them.

For the move into pots a conventional potting compost mixture can be used, with the addition of a little extra peat to lighten it. Fill the pots by gently pressing the mixture into position, then make a hole in the centre with a finger – the hole should be just deep enough for the roots to rest at the bottom of it and for the leaves to be above the surface of the soil when the compost is gently firmed around the seedling Water the pots and stand them so that they are touching one another in a light but not too sunny place.

From then on you simply maintain a reasonable temperature, water as necessary, protect from strong sunshine and give a little fresh air when it becomes very hot Then you sit back and wait for the plants to grow. This they should do at a good pace, and when the leaves are touching one another, the pots can be spaced out just a little. Then comes the testing time when you have to prove your courage – you will almost certainly have far too many plants for your requirements, so you either have to throw some away or give them away, because if you keep them all in an inadequate space, none of them will do very well. With coleus at this stage, your selection can be based on colouring – keeping only the most attractive.

The procedure detailed above for raising coleus can, of course, be adapted for most plants which you are likely to raise from seed.

One final point; seed is becoming quite expensive, so it may be an advantage to shop around for the best buy. I recall the aggrieved buyer of a packet of lithops seed who couldn't find any seed in the packet. We both had a meticulous search and in the end decided that we had found what might have been six seeds, but they could equally well have been specks of dust. He got his money back, but both of us were amused in spite of our annoyance by the supplier's instructions on the reverse of the packet, which simply read: 'Sow thinly'.

Raising Plants From Cuttings

Cuttings can be taken from all manner of plants and the easiest are probably Ivies, pileas and tradescantias – in fact, Ivy cuttings made from two leaves and a piece of stem will root much better if put in the ground outside in a shaded corner during the summer. Adding a little peat to the soil to make it more agreeable will help the cuttings to root in no time. They can be potted into 3in. (8cm.) pots once they are seen to be growing.

Pileas can be put into pots of peaty compost and placed in warm conditions out of the sun. To prepare the cuttings, take a piece from the top of a stem about 3in. (8cm.) in length, remove the lower leaves and trim cleanly just below a joint or node before inserting up to six in a 3in. (8cm.) pot. Put the cuttings into a warm propagating case and they will root in about three weeks. If no propagating case is available, put pot and cuttings into a sealed polythene bag where transpiration will be reduced to nil and cuttings will root very readily. If the polythene bag is supported by one or two small sticks pushed into the soil, this will prevent it sagging on to the cuttings and causing wet-rot problems. Tradescantia and a number of other plants can be propagated in almost exactly the same way.

Whatever form of propagation is contemplated, it is essential that only the best possible cutting material should be used and that the pots and everything else connected with the operation should be spotlessly clean. It is important to maintain a temperature of at least 16°C. (60°F.) with even higher temperatures being preferred by most plants, certainly the more delicate ones. Cuttings should be planted as soon as they are made, and if, for example, a cutting should accidentally fall into your hand when you are visiting someone's greenhouse, it should go into a polythene bag at the first opprotunity. Otherwise, it will go completely limp and have much less chance of survival. But I must say that all my cuttings acquired in this way seem to do astonishingly well!

Increase From Plantlets

The easiest house plant to increase is the Spider Plant, *Chlorophytum comosum*, as it simply means pegging down the young plantlets in small pots of soil and cutting away the stalk that attaches them to the parent plant, at which time they soon make headway on their own roots. *Saxifraga sarmentosa*, Mother of Thousands, is similar, but is better placed in the centre of a box of soil with the young plants rooting into the growing medium with no assistance whatsoever.

Increase By Division

Aspidistras and spathiphyllums can be increased by well watering the soil before dividing the root clumps and potting the pieces individually.

When to Repot

Propagation is a fascinating subject and there are lots of plants with which one can make interesting experiments. Checking to see whether or not plants need to be transferred to larger pots is another job to do occasionally, but it is not something to get obsessive about. Indeed, as I have already said on p. 7, it damages the root system. When repotting is necessary, spring is the best time to do it. Winter repotting of plants growing in a warm greenhouse may be all very well but I would not recommend it for plants in the home.

Plants that come direct from the nursery will frequently require potting on almost right away as they will almost certainly be well established in their pots. But plants that have a few thin roots protruding through the drainage holes in the bottom of the pots are not necessarily in need of repotting. It is often the case that such plants have been standing on capillary sand beds at the nursery (which makes watering thousands of plants very much easier for the nurseryman) and it is inevitable that some roots are going to make their way through to the source of the moisture.

Having decided that potting on is necessary, choose a pot size that is only slightly larger (with smaller plants about 1in. (2.5cm.) all round) as it is most important that potting on should be done in easy stages and that the new pot is proportionally correct for the plant (see p. 72).

The type of pot used, plastic or clay, is usually a matter of personal preference, as there is very little difference in growth whichever is used. But remember that plants in plastic pots don't need to be watered as frequently as plants growing in clay pots. However, I know, as I used to feel the same, that there are those of you who feel that you must put your plants into clay pots as soon as you get them home. If that's what you like, then it's fine, but care should be taken to soak new clay pots thoroughly in water before they are used.

Also, of course, the new pot must in each case be a good fit for the plant's root ball. If it isn't, use a pot which is slightly larger and add some fresh compost so that the roots fit well, and in this way the plant enjoys a mini-potting on at the same time.

What compost mixture to use? The only stipulation I would make is that it should not be heavy and wet, or very dry and light. To list all manner of possible concoctions would seem pointless as there are so many excellent proprietary brands available that have been thoroughly tried and tested. Getting the ingredients to mix your own could well prove to be a much

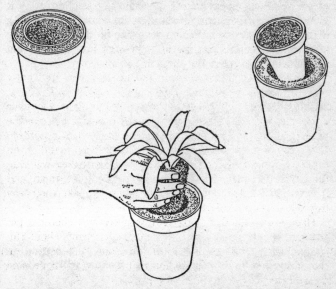

The Davidson system of repotting! A pot of the same size as that in which the plant is growing is placed inside the one into which the plant is to be repotted. Compost is added and the inner pot removed (*top left*). **The plant, now removed from its old pot, is placed in the vacant space and firmed around in the usual way.**

more expensive operation than buying compost from a garden store. However, I would emphasise that compost in plastic bags which have lost their colour and have the general appearance of old age should be avoided – you need a freshly prepared mixture when potting.

I have seen all sorts of potting methods, but the simple one devised by 'Jock' Davidson many years ago, and known to almost every house plant-minded gardening club in and around Hertfordshire, is still the best – or so I think! Certainly the best for the person who has only a few plants to pot and wants to make a good job of it without too much fuss. My method is to have the slightly larger pot ready (it can be crocked, if so wished), put a little soil in the bottom of this and then, on top of this, place an empty pot of the same size as the plant you intend to repot is currently growing in. Make sure that the rims of the two pots are level when the potting mixture has been gently pressed down around the empty pot and the new one. If (as it should be), the compost being used is nicely moist,

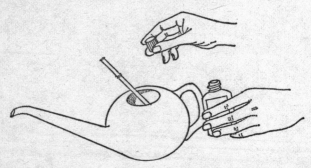

Always follow the manufacturer's instructions strictly when measuring out liquid fertiliser to which water will be added.

the inner pot can be gently twisted and removed, so leaving a perfect mould for the root ball of the plant to fit into. I know that some of you may think this is all a bit daft, but, although I am not a betting man, I would be quite prepared to give reasonable odds that the best potter in the business, working conventionally, could not do a better job than the average person using the simple method explained above.

After potting, water the compost well, place the plant out of the sun for a few days and wait for at least seven to 10 days before watering again – you must keep the plants a little on the dry side after potting so that the roots get on the move to seek moisture in the new compost.

It will not be necessary to feed the plants for about six

months after repotting, as there will be plenty of nourishment in the new mixture. However, feeding of established plants must never be neglected, although, during the winter months, the only plants which should be fed are those producing new leaves, and then with only weak applications of liquid fertiliser. Use the fertiliser as directed by the manufacturer, and don't think that by giving lots more than he advises that you will get better plants, for the opposite is likely to be the case.

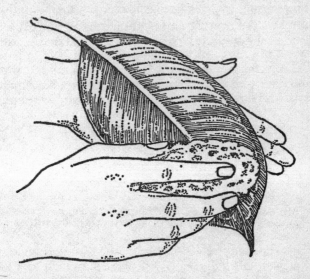

A sponge soaked in tepid water can be used to keep leaves in good trim.

Top-dressing

As an alternative to potting and feeding, many plants benefit from being top-dressed with new compost This is an odd term but it is descriptive for what you do is to remove with a pointed stick the top inch or two of compost (care being taken not to delve too deeply), and replace this with an equivalent amount of fresh potting compost. This not only helps the plant by providing additional nourishment, but it also greatly improves the overall appearance of the plant, particularly if algae has been forming on the surface of the soil.

The general tidying up of overgrown plants is best done in autumn, and is a good time also to prune plants such as hibiscus and beloperone which need this sort of attention to retain a neat appearance.

Leaf Cleaning

Leaf cleaning should not be done too frequently, particularly if chemicals are being used. A sponge soaked in tepid water will usually keep the plants in good trim. There are aerosol sprays that can be used for the specific purpose of improving the appearance of glossy-leaved plants, but it can be lethal to use aerosols that have been manufactured for other purposes, such as killing flies indoors or hair sprays. Hairy-leaved plants such as saintpaulia and platycerium ferns should never be cleaned, except with a soft brush, gently used.

CHAPTER EIGHT

Quick-check Guide

Use this quick-check guide in conjunction with the plant notes which follow in Chapter Nine (pp. 101 to 184). Between them they should help you to decide which you would like to have in your home, office or other place of work.

Perhaps a few words of explanation are needed on exactly what I mean by the term 'good light' as used in the *Light requirement* column in the guide. It is a light position in a room where the light source can be entirely natural or where natural light is supplemented by artificial light. I have indicated where it is necessary to keep specific plants out of direct sunlight.

Name	Decorative Features	Time of Display	Light Requirement	Temperature Requirement	Cultural Category
Abutilon hybridum sativium	Foliage	Year-round	Good light	10° to 13°C. (50° to 55°F.)	Easy
Acalypha (Red-hot Cat's Tails or Chenille Plant)	Flowers	Spring to Autumn	Good light	16° to 21°C. (60° to 70°F.)	Difficult
Achimines	Flowers	July to September	Good light	10° to 18.5°C. (50° to 65°F.)	Easy
Acorus gramineus	Foliage	Year-round	Good light	Hardy plant	Easy
Adiantum (Maidenhair Fern)	Foliage	Year-round	Shade from sun	Minimum 16°C. (60°F.)	Moderately easy
Aechmea (Urn Plant)	Bracts, flowers and foliage	Year-round	Good light	16° to 18.5°C. (60° to 65°F.)	Easy
Aeonium domesticum variegatum	Foliage	Year-round	Good light	Minimum 10°C. (50°F.) in winter	Moderately easy
Agave americana	Foliage	Year-round	Good light	Minimum 10°C. (50°F.)	Easy

				Minimum	
Aglaonema	Foliage	Year-round	Shade	18.5°C (65°F.)	Moderately easy
Allamanda neriifolia	Flowers	Summer	Shade from strong sunlight	Average 18.5°C. (65°F.)	Moderately easy
Ananas (Pineapple)	Foliage and fruit	Year-round	Good light	13° to 21°C. (55° to 70°F.)	Easy
Anthurium (Flamingo Plant)	Flowers	Most evident in spring but can appear at any time	Light shade	18.5° to 21°C (65° to 70°F.)	Moderately easy
Aphelandra	Foliage and flowers	Summer	Light shade	16° to 18.5°C (60° to 65°F.)	Difficult
Aralia sieboldii (syn. Fatsia japonica)	Foliage	Year-round	Good light	7.5° to 18°C. (45° to 65°F.)	Easy
Araucaria excelsa (Norfolk Island Pine)	Foliage	Year-round	Good light	7.5° to 16.5°C. (45° to 60°F.)	Easy
Ardisia crispa	Berries, foliage and flowers	Year-round; flowers early summer; berries later. Very **slow growing**	Good light	16° to 21°C, (60° to 70°F.)	Difficult

85

Name	Decorative Features	Time of Display	Light Requirement	Temperature Requirement	Cultural Category
Asparagus	Foliage	Year-round	Out of direct sunlight	Average 13° to 18.5°C. (55° to 65°F.)	Moderately easy; some easy
Aspidistra lurida (Cast-iron Plant)	Foliage	Year-round	Light shade	Minimum 13°C. (55°F.)	Easy
Asplenium nidus (Bird's Nest Fern)	Foliage	Year-round	Shade	13° to 18.5°C. (55° to 65°F.)	Moderately easy
Azalea (florist's type)	Flowers	Winter and Spring	Good light	10°C. (50°F.) when in flower; generally cool and airy	Easy
Bambusa (Bamboo)	Foliage	Year-round	Average light conditions	Minimum 7°C. (45°F.)	Easy
Begonia	Flowers	Mostly summer but also other seasons	Light shade	13° to 18°C. (55° to 65°F.)	Easy to moderately easy
Beloperone (Shrimp Plant)	Bracts	Spring to end of year	Light window ledge	10° to 16°C. (50° to 60°F.)	Easy
Billbergia nutans	Flowers	Late Winter to early Spring	Average room conditions	10° to 16°C. (50° to 60°F.)	Easy

86

Bougainvillea (Paper Flower)	Flowers	Summer	Maximum light	10° to 13°C. (50° to 55°F.) Autumn to late Winter. 16°C. (60°F.) and above rest of year	Easy in conservatory or greenhouse
Cacti	Flowers and shape	Year-round	Good light	Minimum 10°C. (50°F.)	Easy
Caladium	Foliage	Spring and Summer	Do not place in direct sunshine	16° to 22°C. (60° to 77°F.)	Difficult
Calathea	Foliage	Year-round	Shade from direct sunshine	19° to 24°C. (65° to 75°F.)	Difficult
Calceolaria (Slipper Flower)	Flowers	Summer	Good light	Minimum 13°C. (55°F.)	Easy
Callistemon citrinus (Bottle Brush)	Flowers	Summer	Good light	Minimum 10°C. (50°F.)	Easy
Camellia	Flowers	Late Winter to Spring	Good light	4.5° to 10°C. (40° to 50°F.) Autumn to Spring 13° to 16°C. (55° to 60°F.) rest of year	Moderately easy

Name	Decorative Features	Time of Display	Light Requirement	Temperature Requirement	Cultural Category
Campanula	Flowers	Spring to Autumn	Good light	Minimum 10°C. (50°F.)	Moderately easy
Carex morrowii variegata	Foliage	Year-round	Ordinary room conditions	13° to 16°C. (55° to 60°F.)	Easy
Ceropegia woodii (Hearts Entangled)	Foliage	Year-round	Ordinary room conditions	13° to 18.5°C. (55° to 65°F.) average	Easy
Chlorophytum comosum (Spider Plant)	Foliage	Year-round	Good light	Minimum 7°C. (44°F.)	Easy
Chrysanthemum (Florists' type)	Flowers	Year-round	Good light	13° to 19°C. (55° to 66°F.)	Easy
Cineraria	Flowers	Mid-Winter to early Summer	Light window-sill	Cool and airy	Easy
Cissus antarctica (Kangaroo Vine)	Foliage	Year-round	Shade	10° to 19°C. (50° to 65°F.)	Easy
Citrus mitis (Calamondin Orange)	Fruit	Variable	Maximum sunlight	Cool indoors. Outdoors in full sun in summer	Moderately easy

Plant	Grown for	Season	Light	Temperature	Difficulty
Clerodendrum thomsonae	Flowers	Summer	Good light	13° to 19°C. (55° to 65°F.)	Moderately easy but only temporary house plant
Clivia miniata (Kaffir Lily)	Flowers	Early summer	Good light	Winter temperature 10°C. (50°F.)	Easy
Cocus weddelliana (Palm)	Foliage	Year-round	Light but not too sunny	Minimum 10°C. (50°F.)	Moderately easy
Codiaeum (Croton, Joseph's Coat)	Foliage	Year-round	Lightest possible windowsill	Minimum 16°C. (60°F.)	Difficult
Coffea arabica (Coffee Plant)	Foliage and possibly berries	Year-round	Good light	Minimum 16°C. (60°F.)	Moderately easy
Coleus	Foliage	Summer	Good light	Minimum 13°C. (55°F.)	Easy
Columnea	Flowers	Late Winter early Spring	Good light but not bright sunlight	18° to 21°C. (60° to 70°F.) average	Moderately easy
Crassula argentea (Jade Plant)	Foliage and flowers on mature specimen	Year-round. Flowers in late Winter	Very good light	Minimum 10°C. (50°F.)	Easy

Name	Decorative Features	Time of Display	Light Requirement	Temperature Requirement	Cultural Category
Crossandra infundibuliformis	Foliage and flowers	Year-round. Flowers in Spring and Summer	Shade	Minimum 16°C. (60°F.)	Moderately easy
Cryptanthus (Earth Star)	Foliage	Year-round	Shade	Minimum 16°C. (60°F.)	Easy
Cuphea platycentra (Cigar Plant)	Flowers	Spring and Summer	Light conditions	13° to 18.5°C. (55° to 65°F.) average	Easy
Cyclamen persicum forms (florists' cyclamen)	Flowers	Winter	Good light	10° to 13°C. (50° to 55°F.)	Moderately easy
Cyperus	Foliage and flowers	Year-round	Shade	Minimum 13°C. (55°F.)	Easy
Datura suaveolens (Angels' Trumpet)	Flowers	Summer	Good light	Minimum 10°C (50°F.)	Easy
Dieffenbachia (Dumb Cane)	Foliage	Year-round	Good light but not direct sunlight	Minimum 18.5°C. (65°F.)	Moderately easy
Dipladenia splendens	Flowers	Summer	Light window position	13° to 18.5°C. (55° to 65°F.) average	Difficult

90

Dizygotheca elegantissima	Foliage	Year-round	Shade	18°C. (65°F.)	Difficult
Dracaena	Foliage	Year-round	Good light	13°C. (55°F.) for easiest kinds	Difficult to easy depending on kind
Echeveria	Foliage and flowers	Year-round. Flowering times variable	Good light	Minimum 10°C. (50°F.)	Easy
Echinocactus grusonii (Golden Barrel Cactus)	Shape and spines	Year-round	Reasonable light	Minimum 10°C. (50°F.)	Easy
Epiphyllum	Flowers	Late Spring to early Summer	Good light	Minimum 10°C. (50°F.)	Easy
Episcia dianthiflora	Flowers and foliage	Flowers in summer	Average light conditions	Minimum 13°C. (55°F.)	Easy
Eucalyptus (Gum Tree)	Foliage	Year-round	Good light	Minimum 10°C. (50°F.)	Easy
Euonymus japonicus aureovariegatus	Foliage	Year-round	Light window position	Cool conditions. Hardy shrub	Easy
Euphorbia splendens (Crown of Thorns)	Flowers	Year-round, intermittently	Good light	Minimum 10°C. (50°F.)	Easy

91

Name	Decorative Features	Time of Display	Light Requirement	Temperature Requirement	Cultural Category
Exacum affine	Flowers	Summer	Good light	Minimum 13°C. (55°F.)	Easy
Fatshedera lizei	Foliage	Year-round	Reasonable light	Minimum 10°C. (50°F.)	Easy
Ficus	Foliage	Year-round	Good light but not full sunlight	Minimum 13°C. (55°F.)	Difficult to easy, depending on kind
Fittonia	Foliage	Year-round	Shade from direct sunlight	Minimum 16°C. (60°F.)	Difficult
Fuchsia	Flowers	Summer	Good light	4° to 18.5°C. (40° to 65°F.)	Easy apart from flower dropping
Gardenia jasminioides (Cape Jasmine)	Flowers	Spring and Summer	Good light	About 13°C. (55°F.)	Moderately easy to difficult
Gloxinia (Sinningia)	Flowers	Summer	Good light	13° to 18.5°C. (55° to 65°F.)	Easy
Grevillea robusta (Silk Oak)	Foliage	Year-round	Light shade	10° to 18°C. (50° to 56°F.)	Easy

Guzmania	Foliage and bracts	Year-round bracts spring and summer	Light shade	Minimum 18°C. (65°F.)	Easy
Gynura	Foliage	Year-round	Good light	10° to 16°C. (50° to 60°F.)	Easy
Hedera (Ivy)	Foliage	Year-round	Protection from direct sunlight	7° to 16°C. (45° to 60°F.)	Easy
Helxine soleirolii (Mind Your Own Business)	Foliage	Year-round	Light shade	Minimum 4.5°C. (40°F.)	Easy
Heptapleurum (Parasol Plant)	Foliage	Year-round	Light shade	Minimum 13°C. (55°F.)	Easy
Hibiscus	Flowers	Spring and Summer	Good light	13° to 18.5°C. (55° to 65°F.)	Easy
Hippeastrum	Flowers	Spring	Good light	10° to 16°C. (50° to 60°F.)	Easy
Hoya (Wax Plant)	Flowers	Summer	Light shade	13° to 18.5°C. (55° to 65°F.)	Easy and moderately easy depending on kind
Hydrangea	Flowers	Summer	Good light but not full sunlight	Minimum 7°C. (45°F.)	Easy

Name	Decorative Features	Time of Display	Light Requirement	Temperature Requirement	Cultural Category
Hypocyrta glabra (Clog Plant)	Flowers and foliage	Flowers in Spring	Good light	13° to 16°C. (55° to 60°F.)	Easy
Hypoestes	Foliage	Year-round	Good light	Minimum 13°C. (55°F.)	Easy
Impatiens (Busy Lizzie)	Flowers	Summer	Good light	10° to 16°C. (50° to 60°F.)	Easy
Iresine herbstii	Foliage	Year-round	Good light	Minimum 10°C. (50°F.)	Easy
Isolepis gracilis	Foliage	Year-round	Shade	Minimum 13°C. (55°F.)	Easy
Jasminum polyanthum (Jasmine)	Flowers	January and February	Good light	10° to 16°C. (50° to 60°F.) average	Easy
Kalanchoe	Flowers	February to May	Good light	10° to 18.5°C. (50° to 65°F.)	Easy
Kentia (Palm)	Foliage	Year-round	Good light but shade from strong sunlight	Minimum 18.5°C. (65°F.)	Moderately easy
Maranta	Foliage	Year-round	Shade	Around 18.5°C. (65°F.)	Easy to difficult

	Flowers	Summer	Light shade	Minimum 18.5°C. (65°F.)	Temporary house plant, usually kept in warm greenhouse
Medinilla magnifica			Light shade	Minimum 18.5°C. (65°F.)	Temporary house plant, usually kept in warm greenhouse
Mimosa pudica (Sensitive Plant)	Foliage	Summer to Winter	Good light	13° to 18.5°C. (55° to 65°F.)	Easy
Monstera (Swiss Cheese Plant)	Foliage	Year-round	Shade	Minimum 16°C. (60°F.)	Easy
Neanthe bella (Parlour Palm)	Foliage	Year-round	Good light	13° to 18.5°C. (55° to 65°F.)	Easy
Neoregelia	Foliage and flowers	Year-round, flowers intermittent	Light shade	16° to 21°C. (60° to 70°F.)	Easy
Nephrolepis exaltata (Ladder Fern)	Foliage	Year-round	Light shade	Minimum 10°C. (50°F.)	Easy
Oplismenus hirtellus variegatus	Foliage	Year-round	Good light	Minimum 10°C. (50°F.)	Easy
Opuntia microdasys	Pad-like growths	Year-round	Sunny window	Minimum 10°C. (50°F.)	Easy
Pandanus (Screw Pine)	Foliage	Year-round	Good light	Minimum 16°C. (60°F.)	Easy

Name	Decorative Features	Time of Display	Light Requirement	Temperature Requirement	Cultural Category
Pelargonium	Flowers	Late spring to early autumn	Good light	Minimum 7.5°C. (45°F.)	Easy
Pellaea rotundifolia (Cliff Brake Fern)	Foliage	Year-round	Shade	Minimum 10°C. (50°F.)	Easy
Pellionia daveauana	Foliage	Year-round	Shade	Minimum 13°C. (55°F.)	Easy
Peperomia	Foliage	Year-round	Windowsill but not an excessively sunny one	Minimum 13°C. (55°F.)	Easy
Philodendron	Foliage	Year-round	Shade from direct sunlight	Minimum 16°C. (60°F.)	Easy to difficult
Phoenix (Date Palm)	Foliage	Year-round	Good light	Minimum 13°C. (55°F.)	Moderately easy
Pilea	Foliage	Year-round	Moderate light avoiding bright sunlight	13° to 18.5°C. (55° to 65°F.)	Easy
Plectranthus	Foliage	Year-round	Near window offering reasonable light	Minimum 13°C. (55°F.)	Easy

Pleomele reflexa variegata (Song of India)	Foliage	Year-round	Good light	13° to 18°C. (55° to 65°F.)	Moderately easy
Plumbago capensis (Cape Leadwort)	Flowers	Summer	Good light	7° to 13°C. (45° to 55°F.), Autumn to Spring 13° to 18°C. (55° to 65°F.) rest of year	Easy in conservatory, difficult in home
Poinsettia	Bracts	Winter	Light, sunny windowsill	16° to 18.5°C. (60° to 65°F.)	Moderately easy
Primula	Flowers	Late Winter and Spring	Good light	10° to 13°C. (50° to 55°F.)	Easy
Rhoeo discolor (Three Men in a Boat, Moses in the Bulrushes)	Foliage	Year-round	Shade	13° to 18.5°C. (55° to 65°F.)	Moderately easy
Rhoicissus (Grape Ivy)	Foliage	Year-round	Good light but not sunny position	Minimum 13°C. (55°F.)	Easy
Saintpaulia (African Violet)	Flowers	Year-round	Good light	16° to 21°C. (60° to 70°F.)	Moderately easy

Name	Decorative Features	Time of Display	Light Requirement	Temperature Requirement	Cultural Category
Sansevieria trifasciata laurentii (Mother-in-Law's Tongue)	Foliage	Year-round	Good light	Minimum 10°C. (50°F.)	Easy
Saxifraga sarmentosa (Mother of Thousands)	Foliage	Year-round	Good light	10° to 16°C. (50° to 60°F.)	Easy
Schefflera digitata (Umbrella Plant)	Foliage	Year-round	Good light but shade from direct sunlight	13° to 18.5°C. (55° to 65°F.)	Easy
Schlumbergera gaertneri (Whitsun Cactus)	Flowers	Spring	Good light	13° to 18.5°C. (55° to 65°F.)	Easy
Scindapsus aureus (Money Plant or Devil's Ivy)	Foliage	Year-round	Shade	Minimum 16°C. (60°F.)	Moderately easy
Solanum capsicastrum (Winter Cherry)	Berries	Christmas period and other times of year	Good light	13° to 18.5°C. (55° to 65°F.)	Easy

Plant	Grown for	Flowering time	Light conditions	Minimum temperature	Difficulty
Sparmannia africana (African Wind Flower, Indoor Lime)	Foliage and flowers	Year-round, flowers in May and June	Average room conditions	Minimum 16°C. (60°F.)	Easy
Spathiphyllum (White Sails)	Foliage and flower-like spathes	Year-round flowering variable	Shade	16° to 21°C. (60° to 70°F.)	Moderately easy
Stephanotis floribunda (Madagascar Jasmine)	Flowers	Summer	Very good light	Minimum 13°C. (55°F.)	Easy
Streptocarpus (Cape Primrose)	Flowers	Summer	Good light but shade from strong sunlight	Minimum 13°C. (55°F.)	Easy
Thunbergia alata (Black-eyed Susan)	Flowers	Summer	Reasonable light	13° to 18.5°C. (55° to 65°F.)	Easy
Tillandsia cyanea	Flowers and bracts	Flowering time variable	Light shade	13° to 21°C. (55° to 70°F.)	Easy
Tradescantia fluminensis (Wandering Sailor)	Foliage	Year-round	Light shade	7° to 16°C. (45° to 60°F.)	Easy
Vriesea	Foliage and bracts	Year-round, and bracts in Summer and Autumn	Light shade	16° to 21°C. (60° to 70°F.)	Moderately easy

99

Name	Decorative Features	Time of Display	Light Requirement	Temperature Requirement	Cultural Category
Zebrina pendula (Wandering Jew)	Foliage	Year-round	Light shade	10° to 16°C. (50° to 60°F.)	Easy
Zygocactus truncatus (Christmas Cactus)	Flowers	Winter	Sunny windowsill	Minimum 13°C. (55°F.)	Easy

CHAPTER NINE

Davidson's File

In this chapter I have cast my net wide to include a very broad range of plants for the home, some extraordinarily easy to grow, many needing quite a lot of care and some being difficult but certainly worth persevering with. I have tried to be as objective as possible in my comments, whether the plant in question is one which has been around for many years, or is a comparative newcomer, of which there is a steady trickle coming along all the time. Here goes . . .

Abutilon

The abutilons are comparatively easy to manage and my particular favourite is *Abutilon hybridum savitzii*, which came to me by way of an old friend as little more than a rooted cutting. In three years it has found its way into a shallow tub measuring some 15in. (38cm.) in diameter. The pendulous flowers are sparsely borne and insignificant, but the arching stems carrying pale green and off-white toothed leaves more than compensate for the lack of flowers. Come wind, rain or shine, my plant seems to enjoy standing out on the terrace from late spring to early autumn, when it is brought in to similar light and cool conditions to be overwintered at around 10°C. (50°F.). It must be added, however, that the conservatory or sunroom makes it a better home than rooms that become very hot and airless during the winter months. Given reasonable conditions, cuttings may be taken at almost any time, although early spring is best. When potting on, use a compost that has a reasonable amount of loam in the mixture. It requires ample watering when in active growth, less at other times. The same applies to feeding with liquid fertiliser.

Acalypha (Red-hot Cat's Tail or Chenille Plant)

Acalypha hispida is the plant with 6 to 9in. (15 to 23cm.) long red cat's tail-like flowers that hang from almost every leaf joint on healthy plants, but it is not suited to room conditions for more than short periods. It has green leaves, grows to a height of about 6ft. (2m.) and needs lots of water and feeding during spring and summer. The plant which you are more likely to come across is *A. wilkesiana* (syn. *A. tricolor*) which is more compact and has much more colourful bronze-variegated foliage. Indoors or in the greenhouse the major problem with these is the troublesome red spider mite, which is difficult to detect on the bronze-coloured leaves of the latter plant. Water and feed well (but less in winter), and maintain a minimum temperature of 16°C. (60°F.).

Achimenes (Hot-water Plant)

The achimenes are compact plants which bear flat-faced flowers in many shades and in great quantity. The colours include purple, blue, mauve, red, pink, yellow and white. They are reasonably easy to manage and the flowering period is July to September. The top growth dies down in late autumn and the plants should then be kept in a warm, frost-free place until the following February when renewed watering will quickly start them into growth. Alternatively, at this time the scaly rhizomes can be taken from their pots and divided to make fresh plants. Soaking these in hot water before planting will encourage more rapid growth – hence the common name of Hot-water Plant. Watch the watering and feeding and keep them in an airy place offering good light and the plants will be little bother.

Acorus gramineus

This miniature grass-like aquatic plant is not much as far as plants go, but it provides a little interest if you're using water as part of the plant display. Cream and green spiky leaves are thickly clustered together and the plant is no bother provided it is kept well watered. It can be increased by dividing the clumps at any time of the year.

Adiantum (Maidenhair Fern)

The adiantums or Maidenhair Ferns are marvellous plants, available in many different varieties, with most suppliers giving you several to choose from. Pale green foliage and black leaf stalks provide a wonderful contrast that places these plants in a category of their own. For a showman like myself there is nothing more rewarding in the way of foliage than to see a large potful of maidenhair fern bursting with growth. To do well this plant must be provided with a minimum temperature of 16°C. (60°F.) and have moisture at its roots at all times. Shade from the sun, and if possible keep the surrounding atmosphere moist by spraying over the foliage periodically. Propagate by dividing established clumps. When repotting, use a very peaty compost mixture.

Aechmea (Urn Plant)

Numerous aechmeas are available, and many are among the top layer of cream as far as plants in pots are concerned. Several Continental nurserymen specialise in producing *Aechmea rhodocyanea* (syn. *A. fasciata*) and they have my total admiration for their standards of quality – not easy to obtain with plants that take upwards of five years to mature. This plant belongs to the splendid *Bromeliaceae* family, and has broad, recurving, rosette-forming silvery-grey foliage that is a feature in itself. But it pales to the very ordinary when the blue-flowered pink bracts emerge from the reservoir of water that must be ever-present in the centre of the leaves. Perhaps I am imagining things (not unusual!), but it seems to me that the bracts do not now last for anything like the nine or so months that used to be accredited to them. Four months would now be nearer the mark; but, in spite of the high cost of the plant, this is ample reward from such a show-stopper.

After flowering, the dead stalk should be removed, and in time the main part of the plant should also be disposed of to leave the young growth at the base of the old plant to grow on and flower in two to three years' time, if you are lucky. But when you think how unlucky you could be, you begin to realise just how much homage you should be paying to the

genius of a nurseryman who produces aechmeas of such perfection with so very few failures. The young growths can be
removed and potted up individually in a peaty compost mixture,
but my advice is that better results will be obtained if they are
left attached to the parent plant. Feeding is not necessary, but
a very weak liquid fertiliser will do no harm. The water vase
must never be allowed to dry out, and the soil in the pot should
be moist, erring on the dry rather than the wet side. No attempt
should be made to clean the leaves.

Another special favourite of mine, although in very short
supply, is *A. caudata*. This has broad leaves which are almost
entirely cream in colour; better specimens may have leaves
almost 3ft. (1m.) in length. Not very demanding, this species
requires a minimum temperature of 16°C. (60°F.) and
reasonable light in which to grow. For many years, I took
examples of this plant to the Suffolk Show, as much to please
the wife of one of the show organisers as anything else. You
see, at that time one of its names was *Aechmea forgetii*, and the
lady in question could be guaranteed to have a hearty chuckle
as she asked each year, 'Couldn't you remember the name?'

Aeonium domesticum variegatum

Several aeoniums may be found at flower shows, if you keep
your eyes open, and *Aeonium domesticum variegatum*, with
pleasing variegation, is the one that is most likely to be seen.
Being succulent (they belong to the crassula family), they
should be kept on the dry side, particularly during the winter
months; and they do perfectly well in modest temperatures,
provided there is adequate light.

Aeonium domesticum variegatum, from the Canary Islands,
has a compact, somewhat shrubby habit with attractive
rosettes of rounded oval leaves coloured pale green and white.

African Violet, see Saintpaulia

African Wind Flower, see Sparmannia africana

Agave americana

The best-known of the agaves is probably *Agave americana*

which, when confined to a pot, develops into a plant some 3ft. (1m.) across. It is a fine plant for a dry, well-lit location, but not the sort of thing you would want to take to bed with you – the ends of the bold grey-green leaves with their sharp spines are very spiteful! The strap-like leaves are borne in a rosette. This plant needs no particular treatment, but it will need frequent repotting in its early years and must be grown in a clay pot if it is to retain its equilibrium.

Aglaonema

When contemplating buying a bold-leaved aglaonema be sure to take the precaution of inspecting the plant in the area where the leaf joins the main stem. This is where the filthy and persistent mealy bugs make their home. You may well ask why these troublesome pests are not eradicated before you see them offered for sale, and the reason is that the bugs are protected in an area that is almost impenetrable to conventional insecticide sprays. So, be warned.

There are others, but *Aglaonema* Silver Queen is the plant which is most widely grown, this having attractive grey-green leaves and a compact habit. None of these plants are particularly easy to manage in the home, and they must be given a minimum temperature of 18.5°C. (65°F.), careful watering, and feeding that is never excessive. Shade is appreciated. Potting is only necessary every second or third year, and it is essential to use a peaty compost.

Allamanda neriifolia

Provided it has ample water at all times it is just possible to keep *Allemanda neriifolia* – a 3ft. (1m.) tall plant bearing rich yellow trumpet flowers in midsummer – as an indoor plant. Regular feeding of established plants is also a must, and potting on should be undertaken when the pots are well filled with roots. It is best to use a loam-based potting mixture; in fact, to use a soilless concoction would be a complete waste of effort. Most other allemandas offered for sale should be admired but not purchased as they are problem plants even in heated greenhouse conditions which are near to ideal. There is little hope for them on the windowsill.

Ananas bracteatus striatus (Pineapple)

The green version of ananas, even when in fruit is a pretty miserable thing and hardly worth considering as a decorative plant. But its variegated form, *Ananas bracteatus striatus*, fully lives up to that splendid name, and when four-to-five-year-old plants bear fruit then you really have something for the neighbours to come in to see. And when it is in fruit there is the added bonus of the cream and green variegated leaves becoming suffused with rich reddish-pink. Mature plants are a full 3ft. (1m.) in diameter, have very vicious spines along the margins of the sword-like leaves, and need to be placed well out of harm's way. We used to have awful problems when packing these and taking them to flower shows, but the process is now greatly simplified by the unceremonious process of dropping them into a clean polythene bag and, on arrival, slitting the bottom of the bag and pulling it up, over and away from the plant. Even so, there are a few swear words and numerous scratched arms to go along with the business of packing them.

Grow them indoors in good light, never allow them to become too wet and give them weak liquid fertiliser when you think about it – but not too often or too much.

Anthurium (Flamingo Plant)

The anthurium with long flower stalks, pink, red, or (rarely) white spathes and long, rounded spadix covered with small white flowers, much used by the more lavish flower arrangers and florists, is *A. andreanum*. It is of no account as an indoor plant as it is simply too difficult to manage. The more likely plant is *A. scherzerianum*, with shorter flower stalks, scarlet spathes and curled scarlet spadix; it is altogether easier to care for. Even so, it will need a temperature of 18.5° to 21°C. (65° to 70°F.), lightly shaded conditions and soil that is never allowed to dry out. When potting on (every second year at the most) it is best to use a peat and leafmould mixture. The exotic red 'flowers' are more evident in the spring but are likely to appear at almost any time.

Aphelandra

Whatever has happened to *Aphelandra squarrosa louisae* – we hear of all sorts of endangered species, but who would have thought that this beautiful plant grown in tens of thousands only a decade ago, would now be almost unobtainable? I know, you read about them still in all sorts of house plant books, but one feels that the authors are well out of touch, or have never been in touch! The fact is that you can get plenty of the much inferior, but more compact, *A. squarrosa dania*, but the superb silver-and-green-leaved form with its magnificent yellow bracts seems to have become almost extinct. This I find quite extraordinary, and one must assume that the nurseryman is to some degree responsible, as he felt that the more compact variety could be grown in greater quantity in the same greenhouse space.

One wonders what chance some poor little morsel of an endangered primula species has when growing on a remote Scottish hillside when *A. squarrosa louisae* can disappear from under our noses in such a short space of time. We will probably now discover that there are millions of them about, and that my dark glasses are the problem!

Anyway, aphelandras in general need to be kept warm and in light shade. They must be kept on the wet side at all times and will relish adequate feeding while in active growth. Use loam-based compost when potting.

Aralia sieboldii (syn. Fatsia japonica)

Perfectly hardy out of doors in milder areas, *Aralia sieboldii* (syn. *Fatsia japonica*) has bold and handsome, deeply lobed, palmate leaves. It is raised from seed and grows best in cool, light conditions in a loam-based potting mixture that is never allowed to become too wet. It is also a good plant for use in exhibitions, as it is what I term a 'working plant'. That is to say, when you place it in position it covers a lot of area with its widely spreading leaves. There is also a variegated form, *A. sieboldii variegata*, but it is not only difficult to obtain, it is much more difficult to keep once you have acquired it – a very fine plant, nevertheless. *Fatsia japonica* is the name now valid but I have used *Aralia sieboldii* because it is most likely to be so labelled when you see it on sale.

Araucaria excelsa (Norfolk Island Pine)

On a recent visit to Durban I was staggered to see 80ft. (25m.) tall specimens of *Araucaria excelsa* (Norfolk Island Pine) growing in a more natural environment. Certainly more natural than when this conifer is confined to a pot and placed on a windowsill in a basement flat in Camden Town. But, amazingly enough, quite splendid specimens can be grown in pots if the plants are potted into slightly larger containers every second year using a rich compost mixture which is not too peaty. Good light is essential, but pot-grown plants will need some protection from direct sunlight. Feed established plants while they are in active growth, and avoid growing them in stuffy, airless rooms. It can grow up to 6ft. (2m.) tall and 3ft. (1m.) wide as a pot plant, and with its tiers of branches bedecked with awl-shaped, small, light green leaves (or needles) it can be handsome!

Ardisia crispa

Another plant which I noticed was doing very much better when planted out in Durban gardens is the evergreen *Ardisia crispa*, from the Far East, which grows up to 3ft. (1m.) tall, and has fragrant white star flowers in early summer followed by red berries. Or rather it should have! As a potted plant it is something of a disaster, and I only mention it now as the sort of thing that one should avoid. It may be all very temptingly described in the plantsmen's catalogues, but take my advice and save your money. It is one of the most painfully slow-growing plants that I have ever come across, and is not much to shout about when it matures. Keep it watered, fed, in good light and reasonable temperature if you feel you must have it.

Asparagus

Of the three ornamental asparaguses which are usually available, all have attractive green leaves but quite different habits. *Asparagus plumosus* has delicate foliage and is of rather erect habit, while the glossy-leaved *A. sprengeri* and *A. meyeri* (which is slightly more difficult to grow) have pale green foliage that grows in cylindrical fashion around a central stem. All should be kept moist, out of direct sunlight and in reasonable warmth.

Aspidistra lurida (Cast-iron Plant)

'Men may come and men may go, but I go on forever' could well be said to be true of that darling of the Victorian age, the aspidistra – and they have had a lot to put up with on the way. A dear old lady wrote to me recently to say that her cast-iron

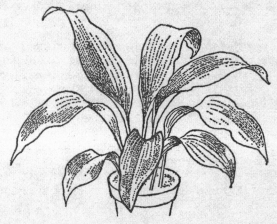

Aspidistra lurida (**Cast-iron Plant**).

plant, *Aspidistra lurida*, which she knew to be over 100 years old, was getting some yellow leaves and she wondered what the trouble was. At the end of the letter she did manage to mention that she had recently split up the main clump to make more plants – it was a bit tough so she used her husband's big saw! The very thought of it brought me out in yellow leaves! This is a tough plant, but it should never be allowed to become too wet, and it will do best in light shade in reasonable warmth. Increase is by division, but try to do it before recourse to the carpenter's tool-box is necessary! Insignificant flowers appear at soil level.

Asplenium nidus (Bird's Nest Fern)

The Bird's Nest Fern, *Asplenium nidus*, has pale green leaves that are arranged in the fashion of a shuttlecock, and it is one of the most beautiful of all our foliage plants. Seen at its best in a pot of about 7in. (18cm.) in diameter, it needs the treatment that is recommended for most ferns indoors – shade, reasonable warmth and moisture in and around the pot. This will mean plunging the pot in a larger container and filling the intervening space with moist peat or moss. Unsightly marks on leaves are frequently the result of slugs having made a meal of them, so preventive measures must be taken. It is inadvisable to clean the leaves with anything other than a soft, damp cloth.

Azalea

The majority of the florist's azaleas originate on the Continent and are another fine example of the ancient art of growing potted plants. Specialist growers export them as more or less mature plants that will be established by the receiving nurseries before being sold by the retailer. In spite of ever-increasing costs they are still one of the most popular flowering plants. On account of their high cost, if nothing else, they are worth that extra bit of care and attention. Looking after them while they are in flower seems a natural enough discipline. But during the rest of the year, while they are in leaf only, there is a tendency to forget them. And forgetting these fine plants at any time will be fatal. Their most important need is water, and lots of it.

Death from overwatering is a common reason for many potted plants failing, so the grower is reluctant to advise heavy watering, but the azalea is different and will be happier if the plant pot is plunged in a bucket of water two or three times each week. There are times when it will need less water, and the best test is to take the pot, place a thumb on either side of the main stem of the plant and then submerge it in water until no further air bubbles rise to the surface. Other than that, keep the plants free from frost and in cool, light and airy conditions. When potting on plants use peat and leafmould as a growing mixture. Care must be taken not to damage young growing shoots when the old flowers are being removed.

Bamboo, see Bambusa

Bambusa (Bamboo)

By way of a change I am writing about something that I confess to knowing not a great deal about, but the few bamboos we have tried have given little bother. One small batch taken to a London department store quickly shed all their leaves as a result of Sahara-like conditions and seemed quite dead, but soaking them with water on their return to the nursery quickly restored them. They would be excellent plants for low-temperature locations where the requirement is for bulky plants which are easily looked after. Ample watering and feeding, and re-potting into a loam-based potting mixture as they fill their pots with roots will keep them in good trim.

Begonia

Many of my favourite plants come under this heading, some grown for their foliage and others for their spectacular flowers. Some are easily raised from seed (the fibrous-rooted *B. semper-florens* is a good example) while others are propagated vegeta-tively, and the largest flowered of all are usually bought as tubers. The specialists' catalogues offer a lengthy list of named varieties of the tuberous kind, and these are the best for the serious-minded enthusiast to buy, but perfectly good results may be had by acquiring unnamed sorts that are sold by colour or as a mixture. Buy firm tubers of good size and start them into growth in February in shallow boxes filled with moist peat; then pot them into a loam-based potting compost mixture when a cluster of leaves have developed. Although they may be planted out in the garden after all danger of frost has passed, much better plants will result if they are in reasonable warmth and good light, with regular feeding once they have filled their pots with roots. As a safeguard, stout stems should be given supporting canes.

Pendulous begonias are grown early on in exactly the same way, but they will obviously be the better for going into hang-ing baskets rather than pots. When well cared for these can be breathtakingly lovely, as I discovered when visiting my home town of Wick in the north of Scotland some years ago. Asked to judge the flowers in the tent at the county show I went along expecting to find a very mediocre lot of plants that had been grown on windowsills, as there were so few greenhouses in evidence. But the reverse was the case – the plants were among the finest I had ever seen anywhere, many of them displayed by the ladies of the farming fraternity. The quality of the blooms and the comments as I did my rounds made it evident that the flowers of the pendulous and tuberous begonias on display were not the result of a chance purchase of a few bargain-price tubers from the local greengrocer – they were all named varieties and some of the prices quoted were quite staggering. If nothing else it proved the point that if you want the best, then you have to pay that little extra in the beginning. However, if you are a newcomer to growing anything in pots it is better to learn with the cheaper ones first to see how you get on.

In recent years the fibrous-rooted Reiger begonias have been making a tremendous impression world-wide and have now become one of the most important summer-flowering pot plants. The first of these to appear were a brilliant red in colour and in Britain were marketed under the name Fireglow, but there are now many other subtly interesting colours ranging from white and lemon-yellow to salmon-pink. One of the most important attributes of these plants is that they are comparatively easy to manage indoors, provided one takes a little care to see that they are placed in a light window position, are kept moist and well fed, and reasonably warm. In stuffy, airless conditions they will almost certainly in time become covered in the white tell-tale powdery spots of crippling mildew. As soon as it is detected mildew should be treated with Benlate fungicide. After flowering the dead flowers should be removed, and when the plant becomes straggly and untidy it will be time to trim back growth to give the plant a more pleasing shape. There have been numerous accounts of plants of this type of begonia remaining in flower for more than 12 months – fortunately, perhaps, for pot plant growers, they don't all last so long!

The fibrous-rooted Iron Cross Begonia, *B. masoniana*, is one of my favourite plants for display in a large container or at flower shows. The reason is that it is most accommodating in respect of colour blending – where other plants will fight with one another on this point, *B. masoniana* will fit in with almost any scheme you care to think of. The common name alludes to the prominent black cross which every leaf carries against a mid-green background. As a small plant it is not particularly appealing, so it is wise to get it into a 5in. (13cm.) pot with the minimum of delay.

The larger-leaved *B. rex*, with its striking leaf colours and patterns will also benefit from being moved into a larger pot soon after it is acquired, as it tends to become very top-heavy in a small pot. Mildew can also be troublesome on the leaves of the *rex* begonia, which also belongs to the fibrous-rooted section of the genus.

What about the prospect of having *B. richmondensis* in a hanging basket? You have never thought of it – or, possibly never heard of it? It is a very fine, easily-grown, rhizomatous begonia, and in my mind's eye I can visualise as I write the glossy green leaves and pale pink flowers of one particular specimen which has been in flower for seven months and shows no sign of giving up. Alas, it is not a plant that travels well, for the flowers tend to drop off, so few nurserymen are inclined to grow it, which is a pity. But you may have a friend who has a friend who does own one and he (or she) wouldn't mind finding you a few pieces as they will never be missed from this fine, free-growing plant.

There are many other excellent begonias which will grow easily indoors, and, in addition to having colourful foliage they will also produce flowers over long periods of the year. Another one for use as a hanging plant would be the rhizomatous *B. glaucophylla*, with red flowers, and for tall and stately plants you could choose from fibrous-rooted kinds like *B. haageana*, *B. lucerna*, *B. manicata* and *B. fuchsioides* – all easy to manage but, alas, difficult to acquire. One day some bright nurseryman may see the possibilities that they present. *B. haageana* is sometimes called the Elephant Ear Begonia, which gives a clue to its decorative brownish-green foliage. It bears rose-pink flowers over several months from late spring. *B. lucerna*, which can grow as much as 6ft. (2m.) tall, has dark green leaves spotted with silver and carries pink flowers in spring and summer. *B. maculata* also has leaves which are spotted with silver and bears occasional pink flowers, while *B. fuchsioides* has small leaves and small pink flowers which are borne in profusion.

Beloperone (Shrimp Plant)

The yellow-flowered species, *Beloperone lutea*, is a far more attractive plant but a little more difficult to grow than the more common shrimp plant, *B. guttata* (the common name comes from the pink to light-brown coloured bracts which overlie the

Beloperone guttata **(Shrimp Plant).**

insignificant white flowers and do have a distinct resemblance to shrimps). But nurserymen do not seem to want to grow that either – the trouble is that it takes up more bench space in the greenhouse, which probably rules it out on cost considerations.

Even the more ordinary plant seems to be on the wane, and

the ones that are seen offered for sale seem to get smaller and smaller. (Perhaps the nurseryman loses his touch with some crops at times.) Never mind, such plants still give a lot of pleasure and are reasonably easy to care for on a light window ledge where they have ample space in which to grow. They must also be kept moist – but not saturated all the time – and the regular application of liquid feed will do them a power of good while they are in active growth. Untidy growth can be pruned back at any time, and firm pieces of growth can be used to try your hand at the mysterious business of propagation. More on this subject elsewhere.

Billbergia nutans

The billbergia is a member of the fascinating bromeliad family, but on the whole *Billbergia nutans*, the one grown as a house plant, is a rather dull plant that produces a few exotically coloured dropping flowers (it has green, blue-edged petals and red bracts) for a short time in the early part of each year. For the rest of the time it is a mass of stiff, dull-green foliage. Perhaps its principle attribute is the fact that it is relatively easy to manage, and equally easy to propagate by dividing established clumps. Average indoor conditions will suit it, but it will at no time set the world on fire!

Bird's nest Fern, see Asplenium

Black-eyed Susan, see Thunbergia alata

Bottle Brush, see Callistemon

Bougainvillea (Paper Flower)

You will never match the dazzling brilliance of the bougain-villeas you see when holidaying in warm climates, but there is no reason why anyone with a little knowledge of plants should not have a go. The average living-room is a pretty impossible home for them, as there is not sufficient sunlight available to do them justice. Think of their hot, sunny Brazilian homeland and try to emulate the conditions prevailing there and you just might get somewhere; but don't buy very expensive plants and think that you are going to fill the end of the dining-room with the incomparable colouring of their bracts. It is just not on, and to succeed you will need a conservatory or greenhouse that offers maximum light and a winter temperature that at no time falls below 10°C. (50°F.). Keep the soil moist while the plants are in active growth and dry from the time they shed their leaves in October until new growth is evident in the early spring. Prune after flowering and use the firmer pieces to make new plants – cuttings are not too difficult to root in a warm propagating case.

Busy Lizzie, see Impatiens wallerana sultanii

Cacti

Would you believe that a recent house plant survey (probably done in a block of flats on Ponders End!) brought forth the enlightening information that the most popular house plants of all were in fact cacti. Perhaps the point should be made that this particular category of plants is so vast that there would be every reason to believe that it is the most popular without the need for a survey.

An obvious advantage that the cacti have over other indoor plants, from the nurseryman's point of view, is that it is possible to cram many more of them into the available greenhouse space, so they are produced in much greater numbers. And there is the additional advantage that they are as easy as pie to grow from seed, so there is no need to house at considerable cost older plants from which cuttings can be taken. Such plants are known in Britain as stock plants while on the Continent they are much more agreeably referred to as mother plants.

When sowing seed, you should sow thinly, and not make the compost too wet afterwards. You should also leave the resulting seedlings in the seed tray or pan until they can be handled safely, when they can be carefully removed and given a little more room in a similar depth of very open potting compost. As they mature into recognisable plants they can be potted into small pots filled with an open, sandy compost mixture and be allowed to make their own way in life.

It is impossible to give general growing instructions for such a diverse group of plants, but in general one should keep them in a light, airy position and water them freely from spring through to autumn; give little or no water during the winter months. Treated in this way you may well be surprised at the number of plants that will flower soon after they have been watered. Although the majority of plants will happily tolerate this spartan treatment, one should exercise care in ensuring that the plants are not allowed to shrivel as a result of excessively dry conditions.

There are all sorts of permutations which could be suggested when it comes to mixing suitable potting composts for cacti, but in my experience the most important consideration is that the mixture should be open so that it will drain freely after watering. To simplify matters this will mean purchasing a mixture that has a loam base and adding ingredients which will assist drainage – crushed bricks, old mortar rubble and sand are three suggestions.

It might seem appropriate to name a few suitable cacti, but these are endless, and the best suggestion I can make is to visit a garden shop or garden centre selling these plants so that a personal selection can be made. (See also *Opuntia* microdasys [p. 163]).

Caladium

From the moment you purchase this most exotic of foliage plants you are going to be in trouble as, if nothing else, it is one of the most difficult plants to care for in the average home. There may be the odd few successes, but be assured there are many more disasters. However, it is a challenge, and a most beautiful plant, which is half the fun for some indoor plant enthusiasts.

The majority of caladiums offered for sale in Europe originate from the swamplands of tropical America, and are exported from there as tubers in the spring to be put into very warm propagating beds filled with peat where the conditions will quickly activate growth. As growth develops the plants are removed to cooler greenhouses to be grown on to saleable size.

There are numerous colours available, but the best is

Caladium candidum which has white leaves with green venation. This species also seems to be the most tolerant. It is wise to select plants of more compact habit and to avoid like the plague those with long petioles and very large leaves. They may appear to be better value for money, but they seldom do as well as the smaller, more compact specimens. Care for them all by sheltering them from direct sunlight, keeping them warm and draught free, and by providing a moist atmosphere around the plants. Supposedly you can, when they have finished flowering, dry off the tubers and keep them in a warm place until the following year with the growing process magically starting again about the end of March, when the soil is watered. But my recent experience suggests that when the foliage dies down in early autumn that is the end of it, unless you have particularly sensitive green fingers. The major compensation is, however, that these are especially attractive plants that will give considerable pleasure during the summer months if they are given what amounts to loving care.

Calamondin Orange, see Citrus mitis

Calathea

The calatheas are plants for the connoisseur. They will tax the skill of every plantsman you have ever come across, even when he has perfect greenhouse conditions at his disposal. Many of them can be grown very well if they are planted freely in beds of very peaty mixture on greenhouse staging with an adequate array of heating pipes underneath that will keep the beds almost at baking point. And this is how most of them are grown on the Continent, before they are transferred to pots and dispatched to their various destinations. However, taking my reputation in my hands, I would suggest that few if any survive the first year as windowsill plants. The window ledge of the average living room is quite simply no place for these tropical plants. However, if you are adventurous have a go by all means, but make an effort to improve the conditions by perhaps providing an indoor greenhouse of some kind where the plants can enjoy a closer, more humid atmosphere. That is what they need. When a calathea comes into your hands it will be growing in a very peaty mixture (subsequent potting on should be into something similar), and you can assist the plant greatly by plunging it to the rim of its pot in moist sphagnum peat. If you are lucky enough to keep it it will in time root through the bottom of its pot and into the plunging medium, but this will be an advantage, so leave it to get on with it.

There are numerous sorts, but the one most likely to be on offer is *Calathea makoyana* (syn. *Maranta makoyana*) which many will argue has the most beautifully patterned leaves of any foliage plant – so, in the end, it may be worth buying one, if only to mention at the bridge club that you have one in the house!

Calceolaria (Slipper Plant)

Produced in countless thousands, these are normally bought as established plants, unless you have a greenhouse in which you can raise plants from seed yourself. With fascinatingly pouched flowers in a wide range of colours they are easily managed if kept well watered and fed and (most important) can enjoy cool, light conditions. The plants should be disposed of when they are no longer attractive.

Callistemon citrinus (Bottle Brush)

The common name of Bottle Brush alludes to the brush-like, bright red flower heads of *C. citrinus* and, when well furnished with these, this plant can be quite attractive. Careful pruning is needed, however, to retain its compact appearance. However, the tendency is for them to become straggly and untidy as growth is allowed to get out of hand. Pruning should be carried out when the plants are not in flower. New plants can be produced by taking cuttings during the summer months and placing them in a propagating case, or they may be grown from seed. Keep the soil moist and the plant in good light and avoid very high temperatures.

Camellia

Exquisite single and double flowers are set off to perfection against the dark, glossy green leaves of the camellia. It is important that the potting mixture used should be of an acid nature, and the plants will benefit from watering with rain water. The best location is the cool conservatory that offers them good light and very airy conditions. They are perfectly hardy, but they would be better for some shelter during very severe conditions.

Campanula

Be they in the rock garden, herbaceous border, or indoors I have a fondness for campanulas large and small. There is something cool and nice about them. In the unused summer fireplace of an old-fashioned Scottish country hotel I recently noted some fine specimens of *C. pyramidalis*. These were single plants growing to some 4ft. (1.25m.) in height and, on inquiring, I was informed that seed had been sown the previous August and the plants potted on as they matured until they were, as seen, in 7in. (18cm.) pots. Grown in a moderately heated greenhouse before being brought indoors they provided a splendid display. They are ideal plants for a large room which does not become too hot.

For smaller rooms, *C. isophylla*, with its plentifully-borne, white, bell-shaped flowers would be more suitable, and this is seen at its best when it is growing in a hanging basket into which several plants have been placed. Keep them in good light, well fed and watered and remove all flowers as they die. Given these reasonable conditions, the plants will go on flowering for many months – from spring to autumn if you are lucky.

Cape Jasmine, see Gardenia jasminioides

Cape Leadwort, see Plumbago capensis

Cape Primrose, see Streptocarpus

Cactus, Christmas, see Zygocactus truncatus

Carex morrowii variegata

Attractive, grass-like plants are always useful for giving a different appearance to groups of plants, as they are quite distinct from the generally rounded shape of most indoor plants. This particular plant, *Carex morrowii variegata* (with white-striped leaves) is hardy out of doors and ideal for planting in very moist areas, around pools and such like. Plants are simply increased by splitting up the older clumps and potting the resulting pieces in small pots.

Cast-iron Plant, see Aspidistra

Ceropegia woodii (Hearts Entangled)

The succulent *Ceropegia woodii* can be raised from seed, or by planting the peculiar hard, round balls (tubers) that form like a canker along the stem of more mature plants. Essentially hanging plants, they have fleshy leaves that are shaped in the form of a heart and are particularly attractive as they entangle themselves on their thin wiry stems around one another. The common name of Hearts Entangled seems a very natural appendage. Pots with a saucer attached or very small hanging baskets will suit them and it is quite common to end up with literally yards of growth. Reasonable treatment is needed in the way of temperature, watering, feeding and the amount of light given. This is not everyone's plant, but I find it rather fascinating and it is sure to interest the visitor who is not very well informed on indoor plants.

Chenille Plant, see Acalypha

Cherry, Winter, see Solanum

Chlorophytum comosum (Spider Plant)

When I give talks on house plants the audience is usually amused when I am asked the inevitable question about what we do with the brown tips of leaves of the grassy-looking *Chlorophytum comosum*, and my reply is that we 'scissor them off.' The questioner really wants to know ways of preventing his or her plant from developing brown tips, but it is my experience of the Spider Plant that no matter where it is grown or whoever the grower may be they are going to have brown tips at the ends of their leaves. But it is not such a disaster as the plants are easily trimmed, and badly affected leaves can be removed as there are always plenty more following on to fill the gap. Keep them moist, well fed, in good light and pot on each year using a fairly heavy compost. As they age the plants

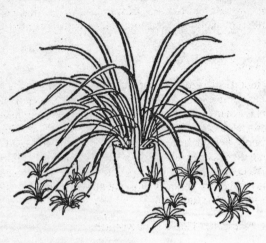

Chlorophytum comosum **(Spider Plant).**

become untidy and lose their good looks, and it is best then to raise fresh ones from the abundance of plantlets which should by then be present. What to do with the old plant? Well, give it to friends and let them look after it while you grow nice, fresh young plants! (These plantlets, strung out on long, curved stems, are of course one of the most decorative features of this plant.)

Chrysanthemum (Florists' type)

There really is not much that one can say about the potted chrysanthemums which are sold in millions throughout the year. Most of them find their way into the dustbin once they have finished flowering, although they can be planted out in the garden where they will grow to normal size and virtually become garden plants of typical chrysanthemum appearance. In the greenhouse of the professional grower they are treated with a growth-retarding chemical which ensures that they remain short, compact and much more appealing as a potted plant. Given good light, reasonable temperature and adequate watering they can be guaranteed to remain colourful for at least six weeks from the time of purchase, if one has taken the precaution of avoiding plants on which the flowers are too wide open.

Cineraria

The cineraria is another florists' flowering pot plant that is inexpensive and good value, as it will carry its heads of daisy flowers for many months from time of purchase if not neglected. The provision of cool, light conditions is again important, but it will only benefit from these if the soil is not allowed to dry out and there is regular feeding with a balanced liquid fertiliser. Keep a watchful eye open for pests, which can be a nuisance, and take action against them as soon as seen. Dispose of the plant after flowering.

Cigar Plant, see Cuphea platycentra

Cissus antarctica (Kangaroo Vine)

For the life of me I cannot understand why this comparatively ordinary plant should have remained so popular as a house plant for so many years, especially when you consider how many much more attractive plants there are which never seem to get a look in. *Cissus antarctica* can also be very troublesome when grown in hot and dry conditions, shedding its leaves in all directions. These leaves are glossy green and toothed along their margins. It is a natural climber which originated in Australia – hence the common name, Kangaroo Vine. Indoors, it likes shaded conditions and reasonable warmth but not too hot an atmosphere. The soil must be kept moist and the plant regularly fed once its roots have become well-established. Grown against a trellis framework it will provide a pleasing background for other plants.

123

Citrus mitis (Calamondin Orange)

My own plant of *Citrus mitis*, the dwarf Calamondin Orange, is years old and stands out of doors most of the time exposed to full sun, coming in only in the winter. It seems to be the ideal treatment if the way my specimen flowers and fruits each year is anything to go by. While outside, it is kept well-watered and is fed regularly with weak liquid fertiliser; watering continues during the winter months indoors, but the feeding is discontinued. Indoors, cool, light conditions are most suitable. My wife makes marmalade from the small, rather bitter oranges, and the plant is really quite a joy – almost like one of the family!

Clerodendrum thomsonae

Clerodendrum thomsonae is of climbing habit, the leaves are dark green in colour and, on the whole, rather dull, but it is a fine plant for growing on a trellis or similar framework for its floral display. A portable framework is best as it can be supported by securing the ends of the canes (or whatever else may be used) in the potting compost. The plant can then be moved around with more freedom. During the spring and summer months the pendulous white flowers with bright red centres are a great attraction and give the plant an entirely different appearance. As a warm conservatory plant it is excellent. It is really only suitable for use as a temporary house plant – have it indoors when it is in flower and in the greenhouse at other times. Keep the plant moist, well fed and in good light, and when potting on use a loam-based compost.

Clifi Brake Fern, see Pellaea rotundifolia

Clivia miniata (Kaffir Lily)

The handsome Kaffir Lily with its glossy green, strap-like leaves and its bold clusters of orange flowers borne on stout stems in early summer, is an odd sort of plant which seems to need large pots that are quite out of proportion to its size. A large pot seems essential as it produces an incredible amount of root when grown in a pot. When potting on use a loam-based compost and feed the plant well once it is established. It is reasonably trouble free provided the winter temperature is adequate – about 10°C. (50°F.).

Clog Plant, see Hypocyrta

Cocos weddelliana

One of the ever-popular Palms, *Cocos weddelliana* has fine leaves and is a very slow growing plant that requires reasonably standard treatment. Keep it warm and moist all the time – don't let the temperature fall below 10°C. (50°F.) – and feed only when the pot is well filled with roots. The growing position should be light but not too sunny, and when potting on use an open compost mixture that contains a good proportion of peat, although not necessarily a soilless compost.

Codiaeum (Croton, Joseph's Coat)

Exposure to cold conditions for even a short time can be quite fatal for these warmth-loving tropical plants with highly colourful foliage. I know this only too well after seeing plants collapse which have stood at Chelsea Flower Show for about a week in the merry month of May. Sometimes they will hang their heads and completely collapse after a couple of days of poor weather; but it is usually after they return to the nursery that the ill effects begin to show as leaves shower off. I tell you this to forewarn you, not to deter you from growing them, and to emphasise the importance of not buying codiaeums from cold premises, which could result in the same pattern of events.

In the home the lightest possible window position is needed, and the soil must at no time be allowed to dry out. Codiaeums also need regular applications of liquid fertiliser if they are to have a chance of succeeding. When potting on a compost containing a good proportion of loam must be used (John Innes No. 3 potting compost, for example). Plants with leaves in many brilliant colours are available, and the apt common name is Joseph's Coat. Mature plants will occasionally produce insignificant flowers from leaf axils, but they are not much to write home about. They need a minimum temperature of 16°C. (60°F.).

Coffea arabica (Coffee Plant)

During the coffee shortage of a few years ago when the forecast was of worse to come, one or two nurserymen who were more than a little astute made hay while the sun shone. They sold coffee plants and, surely with tongue in cheek, boldly announced that one could get so many pounds of coffee beans from each plant. They doubtless failed to add that the new owner should move to Brazil and establish his plant on a sunny hillside, as there is precious little hope of getting pounds of coffee beans from plants that are growing on a windowsill. A few beans, perhaps, but that its about the limit of it – *Coffea arabica* is however, a nice plant with clean, glossy foliage that is decorative enough in itself, but much enhanced when the orange-yellow berries arrive – if they do! Warm conditions and good light suit it well, as do regular watering and feeding. It is also a plant which can take up a lot of space for it can grow to a height of 6ft. (2m.).

Coffee Plant, see Coffea arabica

Coleus

Some of the named varieties of coleus (the plant we grow for its strongly coloured leaves) are marvellous. Those grown from seed are invariably much inferior, but they are colourful and inexpensive, which is not such a bad combination! If you want plants for the windowsill it is best to purchase small specimens in spring and pot them on into larger containers as soon as you arrive home, using a loam-based compost. Some fine plants will ensue, especially if you are careful to select the brightest colours when making your purchase. Coleus are very easy to care for – provide good light, and feed and water well. At the end of the season throw them away and start with fresh plants in new colours the following year. Named varieties will need overwintering in a greenhouse (for preference), and new plants are raised from easily rooted cuttings taken in spring or summer.

Columnea

You can change your mind about plants, and I am now of the opinion that many of these, particularly the more common *Columnea banksii*, and *C. crassifolia* (also known as Firecracker), are very much easier to manage than I had ever imagined. Perhaps the wealth of exotic orange-red, hooded flowers which both of these carry give the impression that they are plants to handle with respect, but they are not really so very demanding.

Columnea banksii.

Some columneas are more troublesome, but the two mentioned will do well in hanging pots or baskets if given conventional indoor care. I should warn you, however, that bright sunlight is not enjoyed by any of them. Cuttings placed in a heated propagator will root readily at almost any time of the year. The cuttings should be about 3in. (8cm.) in length, and the propagating medium peat and a little sand.

Crassula argentea (Jade Plant)

With thick, fleshy green leaves and stout stems, *Crassula argentea* (syn. *C. arborescens*) develops into a fine plant in time, and becomes a bit of a heavyweight when it comes to transporting it around. A little bit of television exposure does marvels for some plants, and this one had a rare boost when it featured on a peak-hour programme with the information that it was a real show winner and had the common name of Money Plant. This led to much confusion when the scramble to buy it started, as the money plant bit must have been an additional name it picked up as it earned its prize money at the show. The old common name of Jade Plant seemed to be forgotten overnight, but the plant is the same!

Crassula argentea is easy to care for; just keep it in very good light and never allow the soil to become too wet. Pot on into a fairly heavy compost mixture, using clay pots as the weight of this plant makes it very top heavy. There are any number of other crassulas, most of which are reasonably easy to care for and more compact than the one just discussed.

Crossandra infundibuliformis

The plant with the incredible name of *Crossandra infundibuliformis* enjoyed a spell of popularity a few years ago, and it is now occasionally offered for sale – perhaps the name puts people off, as well it might. With glossy green, ovate leaves and bright orange-coloured flowers in spring and summer, it needs warm, shaded and moist conditions, and feeding with a weak liquid fertiliser. When the flowering season is over, untidy growth can be pruned to shape but, as it is not the easiest of plants to grow, pruning may be an exercise few will be able to practise! For some it grows well, for others not.

Croton, see Codiaeums

Cryptanthus (Earth Star)

Belonging to the splendid *Bromeliaceae* family, the cryptanthuses are among the most fascinating of all plants, and I would go so far as to say that many of the rarer sorts are collectors' items. Only if you know someone who knows someone can the real gems, such as Foster's Favourite, be obtained. One of the more easily acquired is *Cryptanthus bromelioides* tricolor. Cryptanthus plants have the general common name of Earth Stars, on account of the flat, starfish-like arrangement of the beautifully coloured leaves. They are not difficult to manage

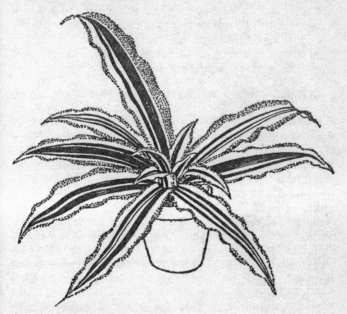

Cryptanthus (**Earth Star**).

if warm, shaded and moist conditions prevail, and they are ideal for bottle gardens because of their slow rate of growth. They are also marvellous show plants if one has time to make a moss-covered bromeliad 'tree' to which cryptanthuses and tillandsias can be attached.

An open mixture of peat and moss makes a fine potting medium for they are not too demanding, seeming to prefer spartan rather than lush treatment with regard to nutrition.

Cuphea platycentra (Cigar Plant)

Raised from seed or cuttings, *Cuphea platycentra* (syn. *C. ignea*) is not likely to set the world on fire in spite of its common name of Cigar Plant. The thin, tubular flowers are scarlet in colour with a white lip, which is said to resemble the ash at the end of a cigar – hence the common name – and they are borne in spring and summer. The plants themselves tend to be thin and poor, and are best when several young plants are put in the same pot and the growing tips of these are removed as the plant matures. There is then a reasonable chance of having more attractive plants. It is not particularly demanding; a light room with regular watering and feeding suits it very well.

Cyclamen

When the florists' cyclamen – forms of *Cyclamen persicum* – are available I invariably have some in the house, as they are to my mind one of the most beautiful of all potted plants. And in spite of the many problems associated with them they are still among the most popular of all the plants that find their way into pots. However, in spite of my long association with these plants and the fact that they have been included in my favourite dozen (see p. 22), I must confess that growing them on from one year to the next using the original corm is one of these little mysteries that I cannot seem to get the better of. Yet I am often asked to judge at flower shows and see the most incredible plants that, on enquiry, I learn are growing from corms which are ages old.

Some years ago one of the gardening magazines actually showed a photograph of somebody holding in his hand a thing that had the appearance of a well-developed turnip. It was, in fact, a cyclamen corm that was all of 60 years old! Perhaps my trouble is the familiar one that once it has flowered and is no longer attractive it is neglected and simply withers and dies. In theory, following flowering, the soil should be kept moist until the leaves die back naturally, and as this happens the amount of water should be gradually reduced until the soil is quite dry. The pot should be placed on its side under the greenhouse staging where it will be reasonably warm and dry.

About the middle of July new growth should be evident in the centre of the corm, and this is a sign that watering should be restarted, after removing the corm from its pot and re-potting it in the same container using fresh potting compost – John Innes No 3, with a little extra peat added to it. The amounts of watering are gradually increased, as growth develops.

I may not be able to keep them very successfully from year to year, but in our house we are real experts at getting the maximum from them while they are in flower. And we do this by having them on the kitchen windowsill where they enjoy full light from this north-facing window. They are watered and allowed to dry out a little before watering again. They are also fed regularly with liquid fertiliser, and all dead flower stalks are removed completely when the blooms are no longer attractive. Good light and reasonably cool conditions are, in my view, the most important factors in growing these cyclamen successfully in the home.

You may keep plants from year to year, but there is no doubt that the most reliable results are achieved by sowing fresh seed annually (see p. 74) and gradually potting the plants on until they are in pots of about 5in. (13cm.) size. From a packet of seed you can expect to get a wide variety of flower colours, all lovely shades that only the cyclamen seems to have.

Cyperus

The smallest cyperus grown is the 2ft. (60cm.) tall *Cyperus diffusus* and a much taller one is *C. alternifolius*, which is about 8ft. (2.25m.). The latter has a place only in very special locations indoors and is more suited to a pool feature at the entrance to, say, a public building. The leaves of both are thin and unattractive, but umbrella-like rosettes of leaves and flowers on top of slender stems are attractive and add considerable interest to otherwise dull plants.

When caring for cyperuses saturation is the order of the day, and they will happily thrive if the plant pot is actually allowed to stand in water. They also need shade and occasional feeding, and new plants are made by dividing the root clumps at almost any time of the year.

Date Palm, see Phoenix

Datura suaveolens (Angel's Trumpets)

In my younger and more impressionable days Angel's Trumpets, as *Datura suaveolens* is commonly called (it bears large white heavily scented trumpet flowers), was much admired and even grown in my modest little greenhouse. But we learn as we get older, and the thought today of bringing one of these fine-sounding plants into one of my greenhouses brings me out in a cold sweat. Why should this be? Because it harbours all the white fly and red spider mite imaginable, and should be avoided unless you have time to continually check the plant and take the necessary action to bring these pests under control. In time it attains a height of some 6ft. (2m.) and will need a large pot and rich compost. It can be placed out of doors during the summer months. When taking it into the greenhouse for the winter it is advisable to cut it back savagely. It will then take up less space and many of the pests that it has harboured will go on the bonfire with the trimmings. Indoors, it will have to have a light position and reasonably cool conditions.

Devil's Ivy, see Scindapsus aureus

Dieffenbachia (Dumb Cane)

The dieffenbachias are among my favourite plants, but the pity is that they do not reciprocate by liking me. I don't mean that they do not answer back when I talk to them (!), it is simply that when handling dieffenbachias I invariably come out in a rash, should I break a leaf or stem and allow the sap to get on to my skin. This cautionary tale should be taken to heart by anyone with sensitive skin – indeed, I would say to anybody owning a dieffenbachia, do not cut the stem of the plant, and, even if you are doing nothing more than removing a dead leaf, wash your hands immediately.

The common name of Dumb Cane is said to derive from the fact that one would be rendered speechless should the sap of the plant get on the tongue. Although I have never tried it, this I can well believe, but due to the abominable smell when the stem of this plant is cut one cannot imagine anyone attempting to make a meal of dieffenbachias.

Despite these drawbacks, it must be said that among these plants are some of the finest of all foliage plants. In *Dieffenbachia amoena* we have a plant that will attain a maximum height of some 6ft. (2m.) with leaves 18in. (45cm.) across and up to 3ft. (1m.) in length – by which time the plant would be growing in a pot resembling a dustbin in size. There are less robust plants and among these the most readily available, and the most attractive with its colourful cream and green variegation, is *D. exotica*.

Many of the dieffenbachias are suited only to greenhouse cultivation on account of their delicate nature, but the easier ones that are sold as house plants will do very well in rooms where the temperature is not allowed to fall below 18.5°C. (65°F.) and where they enjoy good light but protection from full sun. The soil must be kept moist and regular feeding is essential while new leaves are being produced.

Dionaea muscipula (Venus's Fly Trap)

So far as I am concerned *Dionaea muscipula* has a name to fit the bill – Venus's Fly Trap. Its job in life is to catch flies, but few of the plants that are sold are going to live long enough to catch anything – the purchaser, in colloquial terms, is the one who is caught. Few survive, and those that do, of necessity, must be confined to the humid conditions that prevail within a sealed propagating case, as these are the conditions that are likely to encourage the plants to grow – very warm, humid and with abundant moisture. If you must try to grow it, put the plant in a mixture of peat and sphagnum moss, then plunge the pot in similar moss in a propagating case, and cross your fingers and hope for the best.

Dipladenia splendens

A climbing plant with glossy green leaves and an abundance of pink flowers would seem to have the perfect ingredients for success as an indoor plant. But the bother is that *Dipladenia splendens* seldom adapts well to house conditions, seeming to prefer the moister and more agreeable conditions that prevail in the heated greenhouse or conservatory. However, there are the odd success stories, and to have a chance of survival plants should have a light window position and protection from direct sunlight in a room that is reasonably warm at all times, day and night. The compost used must be free draining, and must never be allowed to dry out too much. Feed with a weak liquid fertiliser when the plant is in active growth and provide a framework of some kind to which the twining growths can cling.

Dizygotheca elegantissima

Dizygotheca elegantissima is not an easy plant to manage, but well worth trying as it has foliage which fully lives up to the second part of its name: it is almost black in colour when the plant is well cared for. Buy a young plant for preference, as it loses much of its elegance as it ages. This plant should be kept warm, shaded and moist and be given an occasional feed to do well. Scale and mealy bug are pests which can be troublesome, and these should be countered with the appropriate spray as soon as they are detected.

Dracaena

Only now do I realise that not one of the many artistically appealing and singularly attractive dracaenas found their way into my favourite dozen (see pp. 17 to 26). I apologise to them for the omission! Some are tall, some are short, some have colourful leaves, others are bright green. There is no lack of interest in this fine genus of plants.

The new owner of a dracaena is often perplexed when the plant loses a few of its lower leaves, but this is a natural characteristic of the plant and should not give rise to undue concern.

Of the taller-growing kinds, *Dracaena deremensis* and its many variations is probably the best, and most have variations on a theme of grey-green, with wide or narrow white stripes depending on the variety. Then there is *D. fragrans* with broader leaves of pale green to mustard colour, this attaining a height of some 10ft. (3m.) if the roots are confined to a pot and the top is left intact. The top can be removed if you need to restrict the height.

Possibly the most popular dracaena is *D. terminalis* (syn. *Cordyline terminalis*), which has a more compact habit and seldom attains more than 3ft. (1m.) in height. It has attractive dull red foliage to compensate for its lack of inches. Similar in colour but more compact and needing similar cultural attentions is *D*. Rededge.

Perhaps my particular favourite in this group is *D. godseffiana* Florida Beauty which has smaller, rounded leaves with a yellow base colour speckled with green. If you can stand the cost, several (say three) plants should be placed in a 7in. (18cm.) pot filled with John Innes No. 3 potting compost with a little extra peat added. If they respond to your care and attention you could well have a display which is unusually arresting.

Water these plants with rain-water, if possible, and grow them all in good light and temperatures that do not fall below 18.5°C. (65°F.). Regular feeding with liquid fertiliser when the plants are in active growth is also beneficial.

Dumb Cane, see Dieffenbachia

Earth Star, see Cryptanthus

Echeveria

In spite of my long association with plants I still come across those that bring a tenseness into the system, which indicates that they have something rather special about them. Many of the echeverias are in this category. The succulent leaves formed into perfect rosettes are an attraction in themselves, and a perfect exercise in geometric precision. Some have smooth leaves, while others are hairy, but most of all I think that I like the metallic grey colouring that many of them have. New plants can be raised from the individual leaves that form the rosette, or, as they form perfect miniature rosettes, can be removed and planted in a free-draining potting compost mixture. Keep them in good light, reasonable warmth and

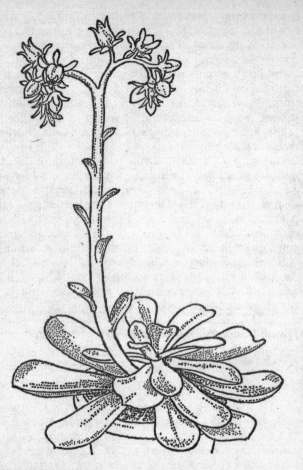

Echeveria retusa **hybrid.**

avoid overwatering and there should not be a lot of trouble.

Plants are not very plentiful, so listing varieties may only lead to frustration. If you are interested in growing them it is better to visit a cactus grower, or one of the larger flower shows, and see for yourself what is available. Illustrated here is a hybrid of *Echeveria retusa*.

Echinocactus grusonii (Golden Barrel Cactus)

In spite of its many vicious spines, *Echinocactus grusonii* is surely one of the finest of all indoor plants, and it is only my loyalty to more conventional house and greenhouse plants which prevented it getting into the top dozen. These spines are yellow, paling with age. It is generally known as the Golden Barrel Cactus on account of its circular shape and colouring but, if I may be permitted a digression, I usually think of it as the 'bird's dropping cactus'. An odd name, perhaps, but it goes back to the time in Dalkeith, Scotland, when a dear old lady told me of the time that hers was accidentally knocked off the window ledge on to the street three floors below. On rushing down to the street there were two traffic wardens with hands behind them standing on the edge of the pavement and looking across the road, so she asked if they had seen anything fall from her window. The reply was in the negative, but they did mention that a bird's dropping had fallen on the pavement only moments before! On turning round she saw her echino-cactus a squashed and watery mess on the pavement – I wondered how the bird would have managed!

Echinocactus grusonii (**Golden Barrel Cactus**).

It is slow growing and takes a long time to reach its potential massive size. Oddly enough, many of the better ones that I have seen have been growing in relatively shallow pans rather than the more conventional full-depth pots which one would consider necessary. Given reasonable warmth and light, the other most important need is that the compost should be free-draining, and that this should not remain saturated for long periods. It is happy in John Innes No. 1 potting compost with the addition of extra sand or grit to improve drainage.

Epiphyllum

There is nothing symmetrical about the epiphyllums, which can only be described as a mess of fleshy leaves growing in all directions, so producing an untidy and generally unattractive plant. But, wait a minute, you enthusiasts, before you reach for your pens; for I am going on to say that everything is worthwhile when the trumpet-shaped flowers in many different colours appear – they are quite breathtakingly beautiful. New plants can be made by inserting sections of leaf, about 4in. (10cm.) in length, in pots, in a peat and sand mixture, at almost any time of year other than when the plants are in flower. They are very easy to care for provided they are kept in good light, are not allowed to become too wet and are reasonably warm.

Episcia dianthiflora

Recently, as I've noted elsewhere in these pages, considerable interest has been shown in hanging plants, with the result that almost any plant that can lay claim to trailing naturally has been in demand. One of these is a somewhat obscure little plant called *Episcia dianthiflora*, which is fine for hanging baskets of small dimension, or pots suspended in string hangers. Interesting white flowers with serrated petal margins seem to be produced with a degree of reluctance as they are never very plentiful. The small, oval leaves are dark green and mottled. New plants are easily raised by removing clusters of leaves (these are, in fact, miniature plants) and inserting them in pots in a peat and sand mixture.

Eucalyptus (Gum Tree)

The eucalyptus is instantly recognisable by the pungent odour that it emits when a leaf or stem is broken. In some parts of the world, where local labour finds the pronunciation of the name difficult, they are simply known as 'Vicks'! The Australian gum trees have established themselves in many parts of the world, but it is the ones with small juvenile leaves, like *E. gunnii* and *E. globulous*, that are best as pot plants. Give them very good light, plenty of moisture and reasonable warmth and they will do well; and place them out of doors during the summer months. Periodic removal of the growing tips will keep the plants compact and more attractive.

Euonymus japonicus aureovariegatus

These fine garden plants will happily adapt to indoor conditions if cuttings are taken and potted into John Innes No. 2 potting compost once they have rooted. A light window position suits them best, and they are all the better for having their growing points removed occasionally. *Euonymus japonicus aureovariegatus* (*syn*. E. japonicus ovatus aureus) has attractive golden-variegated foliage, but there is a tendency for the plants to revert to green and it is wise to remove all green branches as they appear. Keep this plant in cool, light conditions, and never allow the soil to dry out. Feed while the plant is in active growth.

Euphorbia splendens (Crown of Thorns)

The popular poinsettia, the botanical name of which is *Euphorbia pulcherrima*, is discussed elsewhere (see p. 170) but we are still left with a vast collection of euphorbias which could be, and are, used as house plants. However, I have chosen just one and that is *E. splendens*, commonly known as the Crown of Thorns. If nothing else, this plant is abundantly provided with thorns which stand out in a vicious manner from the main stem. The leaves are small and insignificant, but this is compensated for by an abundance of small red flowers that seem to be ever-present. Cuttings are difficult to root if they are taken and put into the potting compost immediately, but they will be much easier to root if they are prepared and left to dry thoroughly at the severed end before being inserted. Light, cool and reasonably dry conditions at their roots will suit them very well, but one must keep a watchful eye for mealy bug getting among the branches of older plants.

Exacum affine

Exacum affine can be raised from seed with little difficulty, and is normally offered for sale by nurserymen from late June. Provided it is given cool, light conditions it will flower over a long period from early summer, the flowers being pale blue in colour and the leaves an attractive glossy green. The flowers have a fleeting fragrance, which is an added bonus. Keep the soil moist and feed regularly in order to get the maximum return from the plant. Although perennial, *E. affine* is better treated as an annual, which entails the sowing of fresh seed each year, during March, in a temperature of around 16°C. (60°F.).

Fatshedera lizei

I often think that the more one fusses over *Fatshedera lizei* by providing excessive temperatures and such like then the less chance there is of succeeding. If the soil in the pot is not too wet it will not object to low temperatures indoors, as it is a hardy plant when grown outdoors in all but the severest of weather. In a large pot it may attain a height of 20ft. (6m.), but the height can easily be restricted by removing the growing tips of the plant. An interesting feature of this plant is that it is a cross between a fatsia and a hedera (ivy), hence the name of fatshedera. New plants are raised from cuttings which may be taken at almost any time of the year.

Ficus (Figs)

The Creeping Fig, *Ficus pumila*, is one of my favourite plants and, as the common name suggests, it is of naturally prostrate habit and is a plant with many uses. In the conservatory or garden room, where there may be facilities for growing the plant against a damp wall, it will cling naturally to the brickwork and provide a pleasing pale green backcloth. Grown in this way the normally thin, wiry stems become much stouter, with the result that the plant is much more prolific in its growth. Damp, shaded and warm conditions suit the Creeping Fig, with dry and sunny conditions being the worst that can be offered.

A simple means of propagation is to allow the growing strands to run over a bed of moist peat so that they will root into the medium – propagation is then simply reduced to snipping off the rooted pieces and potting them up, several to each pot.

The most popular of the ficuses is *F. elastica robusta*, this having superseded the species itself, *F. elastica*, and *F. elastica decora*, which were at one time the front runners – they are all known as India Rubber Plants. At flower shows, through the post and at house-plant talks I still get masses of questions put to me about Rubber Plants, and the most frequent one concerns the yellowing, and eventual loss of leaves. The main reason for this, odd as it may seem, is root failure caused by watering the plant to the point where the compost is permanently saturated so that all air is excluded.

Roots must have oxygen if they are to survive, and if they are allowed to become brown and lifeless then the leaves in turn will lose their colouring and eventually die. So, the main lesson to learn with Rubber Plants is that they should, of course, be watered but they must be allowed to dry out a little between times. Keep them in temperatures in the region of 16°C. (60°F.), in a position where there is adequate light, and they will repay you by growing very much more strongly than they would if growing in very high temperatures.

Potting-on should not be carried out too frequently; every second or third year is quite enough if regular feeding is carried out. Cleaning the leaves is another aspect of their care that causes much concern, and my advice is that you should use chemical leaf cleaners very sparingly. Frequent use of a damp sponge will keep the leaves clean and there will then be no risk of damage.

Ficus elastica robusta (**India Rubber Plant**).

Ficus elastica doescheri and *F. elastica decora tricolor* both have attractively variegated leaves, but are not at all easy to care for. They seem to have a fatal tendency to produce brown marks along the margins of the leaves. This seems to happen in all growing conditions when the plants are confined to pots, and I know of nothing that can be done to stop it. However, there is a crumb of comfort for the enthusiast wishing to have

Ficus benjamina (**Weeping Fig**).

a variegated ficus, and that is the comparatively recent introduction of a variety called 'Europa' which has attractively variegated leaves, grows strongly and does not have the leaf-browning tendencies of the other two.

In order to retain their attractive colouring these plants must be positioned in good light, and a temperature in the region of 16°C. (60°F.) is adequate.

The Weeping Fig, *F. benjamina*, has glossy green leaves and is a very robust grower when conditions are to its liking, but in rooms that offer poor light the leaves have an alarming tendency to fall off in showers. Therefore, good light, but not full sun, is essential, and the maintenance of a minimum temperature of 16°C. (60°F.) is equally important.

Fig, see Ficus

Fittonia

One of the most attractive plants to come on the house plant scene in recent years is the dwarf form of *Fittonia argyroneura*, named *F. argyroneura nana*. This has densely clustered, oval-shaped leaves which are bright silver in colour. It is a much easier plant to care for than any of the other fittonias, but must be given a temperature in the region of 18.5°C. (65°F.), shade from direct sunlight and never be allowed to dry out. It is a very rewarding plant that is little trouble to increase, from cuttings a few inches in length. *F. verschaffeltii* has dull red veining on its leaves and needs similar growing conditions, but it is a much more difficult plant to care for.

Flamingo Plant, see Anthurium

Friendship Plant, see Pilea involucrata

Fuchsia

Grown in a greenhouse or conservatory where there is adequate light the fuchsia could well be my favourite plant, but they are not among my favourite dozen (see pp. 17 to 26) simply because they do pose problems as house plants, as I'll explain later. Plants are available with a wide range of flower colours, some of them more free-flowering than others; but they will all provide a brilliant show throughout the summer months.

They respond well to good treatment, and that includes ample feeding for established plants and potting on into John Innes No. 3 potting compost once they have filled their pots with roots. Keep the plants moist while they are actively growing, and ensure that there is ample light with a little protection from strong sunshine. During the winter months they will shed most of their leaves and they should then be kept on the dry side, with more water being given in the spring when new growth and leaves quickly refurbish the plant. To keep plants compact and shapely they should have their growing tips removed early on.

New plants are simple to raise from cuttings taken at almost any time of year when firm shoots are available, with, possibly, late spring being the best time. Several cuttings a few inches in length should be placed around the outside edge of a 3in. (8cm.) pot filled with a mixture of peat and sand. These will root readily in a propagating case, and will not be too troublesome on the open greenhouse bench, if they are kept reasonably moist.

Indoors, fuchsias are a somewhat different proposition for they have an alarming desire to shed flowers and buds in normal room conditions. This can usually be traced to insufficient light, so it is not only wise, it is essential, that they should be given the benefit of the lightest position in the room. In fact, to get the best display, it is much more satisfactory to have them in a window-box on the sill outside the room. Either inside or out they will need the cultural essentials mentioned earlier: good feeding, potting on when necessary, and moisture at the roots at all times when they are in active growth, with less water being given during the winter.

There are hardy fuchsia varieties, but it is better, unless their hardiness is known, to assume that they will not survive frost conditions, so any pot-grown plants that are outside should be taken in and protected during the winter months.

These plants vary considerably in price and it is worth shopping around for the best deal if quite a few are needed. The easiest way to start a collection is to buy young plants in spring. These are nothing more than rooted cuttings, but they establish very quickly in reasonable conditions, and there is no shortage of suppliers offering scores of fascinating varieties.

Gardenia jasminioides (Cape Jasmine)

Not usually considered a plant for the beginner, the Cape Jasmine, *Gardenia jasminioides* is best grown in a greenhouse or conservatory but it is not impossible indoors if good light can be provided, with a little shade from the sun and reasonably cool conditions – something in the region of 13°C. (55°F.). The stems are woody and the leaves a pleasing glossy green, but the principal attraction is, of course, the creamy-white, double flowers which have very strong fragrance. These are borne in spring and summer. Discoloration of the leaves through chlorosis is a problem, but this can usually be rectified by applying sequestrated iron, available in proprietary packs and applied as advised by the manufacturer. Feed established plants with weak liquid fertiliser and never allow the soil to dry out.

Gloxinia (Sinningia)

With their showy bell-flowers and attractive leaves the glox-inias – more correctly called sinningias – are pleasing plants for summer display. At the end of the season, when the leaves die down, the tubers can be dried off, overwintered in a warm place, and started into growth again in spring. Put them first in small pots filled with a peaty compost mixture and gradually pot them on as they become established. Cool, light and airy conditions suit them well, and they should be fed while they are producing leaves with a high-nitrogen fertiliser. When the flower buds appear change the feed to one containing a higher proportion of potash, which will encourage more and better flowers. If you have a greenhouse you will find that gloxinias are not at all difficult to raise from seed.

Golden Barrel Cactus, see Echinocactus

Grape Ivy, see Rhoicissus

Grevillea robusta (Silk Oak)

The Silk Oak, as *Grevillea robusta* is called, is an excellent plant for the beginner as it is easy to grow and adapts to varied conditions. It prefers lightly shaded, cool conditions, however, to give of its best. Its attraction is its fern-like foliage, which has a silky sheen, and provides an excellent foil for colourful house plants.

Easily raised from seed it is a rapid grower which will quickly attain a height of 10ft. (3m.) or more. But it can be contained by confining the plant to a smaller-sized pot, or by removing the growing tip to curtail its upward growth. Use a heavier-than-usual compost mixture when potting on, and keep the soil moist and the plant well fed – the last-mentioned is an important requirement for established plants.

Guzmania

Belonging to the splendid *Bromeliaceae* family, the guzmanias are typical rosette-forming plants which should be watered sparingly. The compost in which the plants are growing need only be just moist. The leaves are softer and more flexible than those of most bromeliads, and the size of the plants varies with the variety. *Guzmania* Orangeade is a relative newcomer with magnificent orange-coloured bracts and pale green, recurving leaves, while *G. lingulata minor* is more compact with smaller, orange-coloured bracts. They need warm, lightly shaded conditions, and frequent spraying over of the foliage is advantageous.

Gynura

The gynuras are attractive trailing plants that are best grown in good light if the startling purple colouring of the leaves is to be fully appreciated. As the plants age so they become very ragged, and it is often better to strike easily-rooted cuttings at intervals and to dispose of less-attractive older plants. *Gynura sarmentosa* has better colouring and a neater habit than *G. aurantiaca* and should be the one selected, if there is a choice. The flowers smell abominably, do nothing for the plant's appearance and even less for the general surroundings! Remove these as they appear and feed and water the plant well while it is actively growing. When potting on use a mixture containing a reasonable amount of loam. If preferred, several plants can be planted in a hanging basket.

Hearts Entangled, see Ceropegia

Hedera (Ivy)

Almost the first plants that I handled in the very early days of house plants were the hederas or ivies, and I have never lost my affection for them. Perhaps their most important quality is their 'out and in' facility – they can be grown in or out of doors with equal ease, and they seem much more at home in the latter location. This, in fact, gives a clue to their needs when they are grown indoors: they must have cool, airy conditions which offer some protection from direct sunlight. In hot, stuffy rooms there is little chance of growing them well, if at all, and the incidence of red spider mite on the leaves is very much greater in higher temperatures.

The Canary Island Ivy, *Hedera canariensis variegata*, (syn. *H. Gloire de Marengo*), has glossy cream and green leaves and is among the most attractive of plants, whether it is trailing over a wall out of doors or trained to a supporting cane in a cool room. Alas, it is one of the most susceptible to red spider attack, and it is worth while making regular inspections of the undersides of leaves for signs of their presence. These pests are very difficult to see with the naked eye, so a magnifying glass should be used to detect them. When plants are suffering particularly badly the leaves will begin to curl under at their edges and dry brown discoloration will become noticeable. In time, a fine tracery of webs will be noticeable on the undersides of the leaves and in the area where the leaf is attached to the petiole, or leaf stalk. When reduced to this condition plants will require thorough spraying with an appropriate insecticide, especially on the undersides of leaves. Any form of spraying or application of insecticide is better done out of doors, and with ivies it will be wise to leave the plants outside until the infestation has been eradicated. If *H. canariensis* is reduced to this sorry condition you can also consider transferring it to a suitable wall bed in the garden.

All the ivies will reproduce very easily from cuttings taken during the spring or summer months, and there is no need whatsoever for elaborate preparation. My own do extremely well in the shade of overhanging shrubs when they are dibbled directly into the soil. Add a little peat to retain moisture, and cuttings a few inches in length will root in no time at all. Once well rooted they can be dug up and put several to a pot in peaty compost.

In the garden they virtually look after themselves, but in the home they will have to be kept moist and will need regular feeding once established in their pots, but the most important need is that they must be reared in cool, light and airy conditions if they are to retain their sparkle. There are many varieties with attractive leaf colouring and many with interestingly shaped leaves. *Hedera helix* Little Diamond has a name which is self-explanatory, for it has diamond-shaped leaves which are grey-green in colour. It is also a compact and useful plant for incorporating with other subjects in arrangements.

Removal of growing tips will help to keep most of the ivies compact and attractive, but this is not so in the case of one of my special favourites, *H. helix* Gold Heart, which must have lots of cuttings put in the pot initially if the plant is to have a reasonably full appearance. Out of doors, growing against a wall, it will cling naturally and there are few finer garden plants. Many of the ivies tend to produce larger and coarser leaves when outside, which is a benefit with some but by no means with all.

In addition to the few which have been mentioned there are lots of others that are freely available, and all will respond to the treatment that has been suggested.

Helxine soleirolii (Mind Your Own Business)

One of the most practical uses to which *Helxine soleirolii* can be put is as a weed controller under the staging of the greenhouse. There, it will make a dense mat with its tiny green leaves and smother almost everything else that comes along. It is also reasonably attractive, and when the time comes for removing it the entire mass can be rolled up like a carpet and cleared away. From that you must realise that Mind Your Own Business, as it is commonly known, is one of the easiest of plants to care for. It will provide neat cushions of greenery on any windowsill which offers cool, lightly shaded conditions – otherwise, keep it moist and feed occasionally.

Heptapleurum (Parasol Plant)

Under a decade ago we had never seen a heptapleurum in Europe, but from the original specimen of *Heptapleurum arboricola* we already have two variations of this beautiful green plant with digitate leaves and splendid habit. Of the newcomers, *H. a.* 'Geisha Girl' has more rounded and possibly more attractive leaves and *H. a.* 'Hong Kong' is more compact and grows readily from seed.

All of them have plain green leaves, make fine room plants and are very graceful with the parasol-like appearance of their foliage. If the growing tip of any of these plants is removed, it will develop a bushy habit, and if the top is left in it will become tall and slender. Lightly shaded positions are best and a temperature in the region of 16°C. (60°F.) should be the aim. Keep the soil moist, and feed while the plant is actively growing, giving less of both water and fertiliser in winter when growth tends to be less active.

Hibiscus

Like the poinsettia, those tropical shrubs, the hibiscuses, have come into their own as potted plants with the advent of growth-depressant chemicals, the use of which prevents them becoming tall and unmanageable. The length of the internode (i.e. the space between two nodes, or joins, on a stem) is considerably reduced, so treated plants have many more leaves to a given length of stem and are, consequently, much more attractive.

The brightly coloured flowers of the hybrids of *Hibiscus rosa-sinensis* come in many shades and there are single and double forms, but the self-coloured, single, trumpet-shaped flowers are by far the best. There are also kinds with variegated leaves, such as the splendid *H. cooperi variegata*, but these are generally much less floriferous. This particular variety has crimson flowers of smaller size than the normal.

The flowering kinds that are most commonly seen are the *H. rosa-sinensis* hybrids first alluded to, these having fresh green leaves, which may be slightly toothed or plain around their margins, and a capacity for producing an incredible

Hibiscus rosa-sinensis.

number of flowers during the spring and summer months. Individually, the flowers last for only one day, but it is seldom that there is not a new bud waiting to replace the one that has done its duty. Dead flowers should be removed to prevent them falling on to the leaves and causing them to rot. A position in full light is absolutely essential if the plants are to give real satisfaction; and full sun will do no harm if the soil is not allowed to dry out. Feeding is also important, and plants that seem large for their growing pots when acquired may be better if they are transferred to larger pots without delay, using John Innes No. 3 potting compost as these are greedy plants when it comes to feeding.

Loss of some leaves during the darker winter months is almost inevitable, and plants may even shed all their leaves. Those that do can be allowed to dry out and be treated as dormant plants until new growth starts in the spring, when watering should restart.

Hippeastrum

When those handsome plants the hippeastrums (also known, incorrectly, as amaryllises) have leaves, water and feed them well, and when the leaves die down naturally keep them bone-dry in a warm place and forget about them. When new growth is seen after the dormant period the compost should be watered and the plant be brought back into circulation. Top-dressing around the bulb with fresh potting mixture (John Innes No. 3 potting compost) will do no harm and improve the look of the plant. This is exactly what I did last winter with one of my own bulbs and the result was quite astonishing – it produced a 3ft. (1m.)-tall spike from which emerged four spectacular red trumpet-shaped flowers. I thought the plant was then going out of its mind when another spike appeared and grew to a height only a few inches less than the first one, and in turn produced three more flowers. The leaves followed and the plant was kept indoors until the weather improved and was then placed in a sheltered spot outside where it is watered and fed in order to nourish the bulb for the following season.

But you never can tell with hippeastrums – I could follow exactly the same cultural pattern next year and get no flowers at all. The temptation to pot the bulbs into large pots should be resisted as the resultant plant will not necessarily be much better for it and may well rot in the larger mass of compost.

Hot-water Plant, see Achimenes

Hoya (Wax Plant)

In spite of its exquisite pink and white, wax-like flowers, the climbing *Hoya carnosa* is in my view little more than a rampant cultivated weed which in time becomes an ideal home for mealy bug. This pest then becomes almost impossible to eradicate as it finds its way in among the tightly entwined stems. But if you must have one, then it should enjoy good light and reasonable warmth; and it will respond to moist conditions and regular feeding and repotting into a larger pot every other year. If *H. carnosa* settles down to your conditions then it will grow at a prodigious pace and will certainly need to be provided with some form of framework to which the growths can be tied as it curls menacingly out in search of support. It is easily propagated from cuttings.

An infinitely better plant that will tax the growing skills of all indoor plant enthusiasts is *Hoya bella*. This is of compact habit and essentially a trailing plant. The exquisite white and crimson, waxy-textured flowers hang in clusters and need to be looked up into to be fully appreciated, for the individual flowers have a jewel-like quality and, when set together, have few peers. However, the plant is not easily obtainable and it would need the special care of the experienced plant enthusiast to succeed. Hanging baskets filled with peaty compost make the ideal container, and it must be located in a lightly shaded spot in temperatures that average around 16°C. (60°F.). Should the normally pale green leaves take on a hard brown appearance you should immediately suspect the presence of red spider mite and take the appropriate action.

Hydrangea

Hydrangeas in the shape of the Hortensia varieties of *Hydrangea macrophylla* are other 'in-and-out' plants that are usually purchased in the spring and enjoyed indoors before being planted in the garden when weather conditions have improved sufficiently for them to go outside. A word on planting outdoors – prepare the site by digging it over and incorporating some general fertiliser, and be sure that the location offers some protection from late spring frosts, which will damage the flower buds and may well completely eliminate the expected display of blooms.

Indoors, the most important single requirement of any hydrangea that is growing in a pot is that it should be copiously watered. Normally I am terrified of the consequences when I advise anyone to water their plants well as it generally means that the poor things begin to feel that they are in a paddy field. But, with hydrangeas, provided they are not actually standing in water all the time, it is essential that the compost should never be allowed to dry out while the plant is producing leaves. Water is not needed while the plant is naturally dormant, and the minimum temperature provided during the winter should be about 7°C. (44°F.).

Cuttings with two pairs of leaves can be rooted in gentle heat in a propagating case in March or April, and the best plants are produced from cuttings taken from blind rather than flowering stems.

Hypocyrta glabra (Clog Plant)

Hypocyrta glabra is a neat little plant with evergreen, glossy leaves and long-lasting orange-coloured flowers. It is a nice plant for growing in small hanging pots which will show off the flowers to full advantage. It needs reasonable warmth and shade from direct sunlight. A well-drained peaty compost is best, and this should never be allowed to become too wet.

Cuttings about 3in. (8cm.) in length from which the lower leaves have been removed can be tried in a heated propagator, but be warned that they are not the easiest to root. Feeding with weak liquid fertiliser during the summer months will do no harm, and untidy growth can be trimmed at almost any time to make the plant shapely.

Hypoestes

Hypoestes are plants with green, pink-spotted leaves, and they become untidy and less attractive as they age. *Hypoestes sanguinolenta* is the one usually grown, but I have recently seen an improved form with a flush of dusty pink colouring, which it retains when grown in full light but which fades quite quickly in poorly lit situations. Its name is *H. sanguinolenta* Splash. It is very easy to manage if it is kept moist, well fed and in a reasonable temperature.

Impatiens wallerana sultanii (Busy Lizzie)

Commonly named Busy Lizzie, the impatiens are indeed very busy plants which will grow apace in good light and reasonable warmth, if they are kept fairly moist and well fed. Heavier potting mixtures suit the impatiens best, and they must have good light and fresh air if their full flowering potential is to be enjoyed. The one normally grown is *Impatiens wallerana sultanii*, with flowers from orange and scarlet to magenta, pink and white in colour, and there is also a variety named *I. w. petersiana* with red flowers and dark foliage. Cuttings root with little trouble, either in water or, more conventionally, in small pots filled with a growing compost rather than a mixture intended for cuttings. Keep a watchful eye open for pests, as the soft, succulent stems seem to have a particular attraction for them.

Indoor Lime, see Sparmannia africana

Iresine herbstii

Another plant which would much rather be cool than hot is the iresine. The glossy leaves of *Iresine herbstii* are of an unusual red colour and the plant enjoys good light. It will do best if potted into a 5in. (13cm.) pot as soon as purchased – if not in that size of pot already, of course. Water and feed as you would any reasonably easy plant indoors. Grow in John Innes No. 2 potting compost. (Cuttings are not difficult to root.)

Isolepis gracilis

Have this little baby, *Isolepis gracilis* (syn. *Scripus cernuus*), in your collection of house plants and it will be sure to attract attention, as it is quite different to the general run of plants. For one thing, the plant in its pot, can stand in a dish of water, as it is a miniature bullrush. Hollow stems have tiny white flowers at their tips and give the plant an unusual appearance as they droop from the pot and hang down for a foot or more. It will be happy in average room conditions if it is provided with shade. Raise new stock by dividing older clumps.

Ivy, see Hedera

Ivy, Grape, see Rhoicissus

Jade Plant, see Crassula argentea

Jasmine, see Jasminum polyanthum

Jasmine, Madagascar, see Stephanotis floribunda

Jasminum polyanthum (Jasmine)

As far as Jasmines for the home are concerned, the most important is *Jasminum polyanthum*, which normally is a tangled mass of evergreen leaves on twining stems but which in January and February produces clusters of heavily scented white flowers. If the plant you buy has made reasonable growth it will be better for going into a larger pot, using John Innes No. 3 potting compost with a little peat added. To keep the vigorous growth under control it will be necessary to attach it to some sort of framework.

Jasmines are normally fine plants for the frost-free conservatory, and they will do perfectly well out of doors during the less inclement months of the year. Water and feed them well when established.

Joseph's Coat, see Codiaeum

Kaffir Lily, see Clivia miniata

Kalanchoe

The fresh green leaves of kalanchoes have a fleshy feel to them, and are not in themselves especially attractive. However, the red, pink or orange flower heads that are produced over a long period and carried boldly on strong stems are attractive, and these make neat windowsill plants. In addition, they are much used for adding colour to mixed arrangements during the bleaker months of the year. Feed the plants occasionally and water sparingly to get the best results.

New plants may be raised from seed sown in the spring, or from 3in. (8cm.) long cuttings taken from non-flowering growths in spring or summer.

Kangaroo Vine, see Cissus antarctica

Kentia fosteriana

The Kentia palm most frequently encountered is the graceful *Kentia fosteriana* (its latest name is *Howeia fosteriana*, but it is still best known as this) which has dark green much-segmented leaves borne on upright stems. It is graceful, much sought after and expensive! That is reason enough on its own why kentia palms must be carefully tended. This will mean temperatures of not less than 18.5°C. (65°F.), good light but shade from strong sunlight, and compost that drains freely when watered. Give the plants a thorough watering and allow the compost to dry out a little before the next application. Feeding should never be excessive, and it is, therefore, better to give weak liquid fertiliser regularly rather than heavy doses infrequently.

Having said that we now come to the cause of most trouble with palms in general, and that is the use of chemical concoctions for cleaning their leaves – a moist sponge will not impart a glossy sheen when cleaning leaves, but it will be very much better for the well-being of the plant.

New plants are raised from seed, but this seed is not easy for the home gardener to obtain as there is an almost permanent world shortage. When potting on kentias, use John Innes No. 2 potting compost for plants being moved to small pots and J.I.

Kentia fosteriana.

No. 3 for those which need moving into larger-sized pots. Potting on is only necessary every second or third year.

Ladder Fern, see Nephrolepis exaltata

Maidenhair Fern, see Adiantum

Madagascar Jasmine, see Stephanotis floribunda

Maranta

The two most popular marantas for use as house plants are *M. leuconeura kerchoveana* and *M. leuconeura erythrophylla* (syn. *M. l. tricolor*). Both need shady conditions and temperatures in the region of 18.5°C. (65°F.) to do well. *M. leuconeura erythrophylla* has intricately patterned reddish-brown leaves while *M. leuconeura kerchoeveana* has pale green leaves with numerous darker blotches on either side of the midrib.

New plants are propagated from cuttings made from growths which are left, after preparation, with two or three leaves, and the severed ends of the cuttings are treated with rooting powder before being inserted in pure sphagnum peat, either in shallow boxes or small pots. The warm, close conditions of a propagating case are then needed until such time as the cuttings have rooted. Water and feed established plants in moderation.

Medinilla magnifica

Medinilla magnifica is a luxury plant if ever there was one. It has dark green, slightly recurving leaves that are attached to stout stems which are almost square in shape. Shell-pink, pendulous flowers which hang in clusters not unlike ripening grapes are its principal attraction. In agreeable conditions these fine plants will flower continuously. But, alas, it is not an easy plant to obtain and it is really only a temporary house plant, being brought indoors when in flower and kept in a warm greenhouse at other times. A minimum temperature of around 18.5°C. (65°F.) is essential, and the growing atmosphere must be moist, as must the compost it is growing in.

Mimosa pudica (Sensitive Plant)

From a luxury plant to a fun plant: *Mimosa pudica* is commonly called the Sensitive Plant because of its odd characteristic of going completely limp when the fern-like, feathery leaves are touched. For this reason it is not a popular plant with the commercial grower as it is so difficult to present plants which do not seem to be little more than limp rags when they are being moved to market. It is an interesting plant nevertheless, and very easily raised from seed sown in the spring. Perennial in habit, it is, however, better treated as an annual – seeds are sown in warmth in March – and disposed of when it becomes leggy and unattractive late in the year. Keep it moist, well fed and in good light conditions.

Mind Your Own Business, see Helxine soleirolii

Money Plant, see Scindapsus aureus

Monstera (Swiss Cheese Plant)

The monsteras would seem to have everything expected of good house plants. They have naturally glossy leaves of attractive shape, and as they increase in size they have the interesting facility of producing aerial roots which present a perplexing problem for the less well-informed house plant grower. They are also fairly easy to manage indoors. But to return for a moment to those aerial roots – in the plants' natural jungle environment these assist them to climb trees so that leaves can get to the light; and they can also be used by the plant to take in moisture and nourishment.

Monstera deliciosa is the spreading plant with the deeply cut, very large leaves and this is only suitable for large rooms or offices. *M. pertusa borsigiana* has much smaller leaves and a more upright, compact habit of growth and is a better choice for ordinary room conditions.

Arum-type spathes of cream colouring are borne by more mature specimens of both kinds, these being followed by cylindrical fruits (edible when ripe).

To help plants growing in pots we usually insert in the

compost a plastic tube that is bound around with sphagnum moss. The moss is supposed to be kept wet, with the idea that the aerial roots of the plant can entwine themselves around the mossed support and keep the plant upright. Bearing this in mind you can imagine my disbelief when someone telephoned recently to ask when they could expect the mossy thing in the middle of the plant to start to grow! Too many roots can appear untidy and it will do no damage to remove a proportion of them, but it is unwise to be too drastic. It is really much better to wrap the roots around a mossed support, or to tie them neatly in to the stem of the plant and to push their ends into the soil when long enough.

To achieve success, keep monsteras warm, shaded and moist and when potting use John Innes No. 3 potting compost to which a good third by volume of fresh sphagnum peat has been added. The best monstera plants are all grown from seed, which can be sown at any time in warm, moist conditions.

Moses in the Bulrushes, see Rhoeo discolor

Mother-in-Law's Tongue, see Sansevieria trifasciata laurentii

Mother of Thousands, see Saxifraga

Neanthe bella (Parlour Palm)

With pale to dark green leaves (the actual colour depending on the amount of light reaching the growing area), *Neanthe bella* (syn. *Chamaedonea elegans*) is commonly called the Parlour Palm. Growth is very slow, so it is well suited for growing in indoor growing cases and in larger bottle gardens, but it is frequently seen at its best when growing in what would appear to be oversize pots filled with a mixture of sieved leaf-mould and peat. Keep this plant in good light but out of direct sunlight and water and feed moderately.

New plants are raised from seed sown and germinated in a high temperature (about 27°C. [80°F.]). These plants should never at any time be subjected to low temperatures. Clean the leaves with a sponge which has been moistened in water. The presence of red spider will turn the leaf colouring to a hard, sickly yellow and this pest should be dealt with immediately its presence is detected.

Neoregelia

These bromeliads are great favourites of mine, with their tough disposition, spectacular colouring (cream, pink, red and green) and the radiating formation of their exotic-looking leaves. They have, indeed, the typical bromeliad rosette formation with the largest leaves perhaps 3in. (8cm.) wide and up to 18in. (45cm.) long, and have small but vicious spines along their entire margins. For display purposes they simply shout out to be used in the most startling manner, and I love to see them attached to old tree branches so that they have a more natural appearance, for this is much as they grow in nature. This way you look directly into the centre of the rosette. The small blue flowers are insignificant, but as they appear the short leaves in the centre of the plant change to a brilliant red colouring that is seldom, if ever, seen in other plants.

Look after them by keeping the rosette centre filled with water and the soil just moist – feeding is not really important. A lightly shaded position in reasonable warmth will suit them, and when potting on use a mixture of peat and sieved leaf-mould, keeping in mind that good drainage is very important. After flowering the main rosette will die naturally and should be cut away when no longer attractive, with care being taken not to damage the new growth which will be appearing around the stump of the older section of the plant. As soon as they are large enough the small plants can be potted up individually, or left attached to form an attractive cluster of plants around the old trunk. This treatment is reasonably typical of all the bromeliads which form their leaves in a flat rosette.

Nephrolepis exaltata (Ladder Fern)

Our Victorian forebears knew something about grandeur, and the Ladder Fern, *Nephrolepis exaltata*, in its many forms, was one of their special favourites when it came to plants in the home and conservatory. To my way of thinking nephrolepises are essentially individuals, and they are at their best when placed on a pedestal or suspended from the ceiling where they can be appreciated from all angles. The best way of starting is to acquire a full sort of plant in a 5in. (13cm.) size pot in the springtime and to pot it into a 7in. (18cm.) pot, using a peaty compost mixture, shortly after you get it home. In a warm room where it can enjoy light shade you will be amazed at the way in which this superb plant can uncurl its soft evergreen fronds.

Water the plants well during the spring and summer months and keep moist, avoiding overwet conditions during the winter. Plants should also be fed when they are growing more actively, and I often find that they react much more favourably to foliar feeding than they do to more conventional feeding through their roots. Cleaning the leaves is an impossible task, but during the summer healthy plants will not object to being placed out of doors and having their leaves thoroughly sprayed over with tepid water. Low temperatures, exposure to bright sunlight and dry conditions are their worst enemies.

Norfolk Island Pine, see Araucaria excelsa

Oplismenus hirtella variegatus

Oplismenus hirtella variegatus resembles a tradescantia (the leaves are green and silver in colour with pink markings), but it is in fact a grass that is much more straggly and untidy and a difficult plant to control in the greenhouse once it gets under way – at one stage it became such a tangle of foliage I had it re-christened 'opelessmenace'!

It is very easy to manage if given ample moisture in and around the pot, an occasional feed and a light position in a warm room. New plants can be made from almost any piece that breaks off. It doesn't have a common name, which is a pity in view of its botanical name!

Opuntia microdasys

Children are generally very fond of cacti and the opuntias are among their favourites, especially the various forms of *O. microdasys* with firm pads of growth that emerge one from the other as the plants develop. Care should be taken to protect your fingers from the prickly clusters that abound all over the plant, particularly when you have propagation in mind. To increase plants the individual pads of growth are removed and left for a few hours to dry before being placed upright in a free-draining compost mixture which contains a liberal amount of sharp sand. Keep the compost dry during the winter and water fairly freely at other times, but ensure that the water drains sharply through the mixture when it is poured on to the surface. Other than that, a sunny window position in a warm room is all that they require.

Orange, Calamondin, see Cistus

Palm, Date, see Phoenix

Palm, Parlour, see Neanthe bella

Pandanus (Screw Pine)

The Screw Pines are majestic plants that may grow 10ft. (3m.) tall and much the same width when their roots are confined to large pots, but they are slow growing, so it is some years before they start pushing off the ceiling! All have vicious spines along the margins and on the undersides of their leaves, and are best suited to more isolated locations.

Pandanus utilis has pale green leaves and a markedly twisted stem; *P. sanderi* has bright creamy-yellow leaf colouring, and the more compact *P. veitchii* has leaves attractively striped green and white. Broad, tapering leaves radiate from a central stem. The plants need good light, reasonable warmth and adequate watering and feeding during spring and summer; and when potting on the use of John Innes No. 3 potting compost and heavy clay pots is essential. They are magnificent plants for large exhibits, and it is worth looking out for them being used in this capacity, but getting a really large plant wrapped in paper, string, polythene and goodness knows what else is like bagging up a pair of untrained porcupines – the pandanus never seems to want to do what you have in mind for it. One of my favourite memories of staging pandanus was at Liverpool

Show some years ago when a truly magnificent specimen of *P. sanderi* was placed at the end of a large pond so that there was not only the pleasure of seeing the plant but also the bonus of having its reflection in the water. The supreme compliment came from the head at Liverpool's fine botanic garden, who thought it was the finest plant he had ever clapped eyes on. Getting the plant from just north of London to Liverpool was, in itself, no mean achievement. I've gone on a bit about this plant, but it is one of my special favourites – and it is a pity it is in short supply!

Paper Flower, see Bougainvillea

Parasol Plant, see Heptapleurum

Parlour Palm, see Neanthe bella

Pelargonium

There are several types of pelargonium – the zonals with dark marking on their leaves and brilliant flowers throughout the summer months, the regals with their green undulating leaves and masses of clustered flower heads (which make excellent pot plants), and the trailing varieties with both green and variegated leaves which are superb as basket or window-box plants.

Good light is their most important need, with ample watering and feeding during the summer months and no feeding and very little water in winter. Cuttings of firm shoots a few inches long can be taken at almost any time during the spring or summer, and the ends should be allowed to dry thoroughly before they are inserted in the rooting compost (John Innes No. I potting compost). They are really very little trouble if one simply wants a few extra plants for the garden, and can even be rooted in the garden in a corner that is not exposed to too much sunlight.

Frost can quickly put an end to them, so they must be taken indoors before they are likely to suffer damage. Keep them warm and very much on the dry side over winter, starting them into growth in early spring. The regal pelargoniums are much favoured by whitefly, so a careful watch must be kept for these on the undersides of leaves and remedial action taken without delay.

Pellaea rotundifolia (Cliff Brake Fern)

If the nephrolepis is king of the castle among the larger ferns its prostrate-growing relation, *Pellaea rotundifolia*, one of the Cliff Brake Ferns, must be well up among the leaders as far as the smaller-growing plants are concerned. With densely clustered, dark green, almost black leaves it is an excellent foil plant when a collection is being put together of different house plants. Give it the conventional fern treatment of shade, warmth and moisture, and it will prove to be most rewarding.

Pellionia daveauana

That odd name, *Pellionia daveauana*, gives me terrible problems at flower shows when the least interesting part of the day arrives and the labels have to be written out. I find it difficult to believe that there can be so many vowels in one word. To do well this creeping plant must have very warm, shaded and moist conditions, and it is at its best when grown as a trailer. As the amount of light available to the plant varies, so the colour of the oval to lance-shaped leaves also changes from pale green to dark green, sometimes with attractive tinges of pink. It is very easily propagated in warm, moist conditions at any time of the year – pieces of almost any size will happily root in a peaty compost mixture.

Peperomia

How these little plants retain their popularity year after year is a complete mystery to me. They have been with us as front-line house plants for a quarter of a century, yet the cream and green variegated *P. magnoliaefolia* is the only one that one would list as attractive, perhaps, with the less frequently seen *P. sandersii* (illustrated on p. 48) which has rounded leaves with a silvery-green base colouring overlaid with dark green stripes. The other two that are sold in large quantities are *P. caperata*, with dark green crinkled foliage, and *P. hederaefolia* with dark grey, metallic colouring. Both of these are interesting, but that is about all that can be said for them.

None of them will ever make large plants, so they are fine for the windowsill, provided it is not excessively sunny. Keep them reasonably warm, on the dry side all the time and feed occasionally. When potting on into larger pots use a soilless compost and pots that are only a little larger than the ones the plants are growing in at the present time.

Philodendron

Here you get everything: plants which are large, small, difficult, easy, attractive, ugly, dull and quite magnificent. In the last-mentioned category I would put *P. hastatum* (which is very similar if not the same as *P. tuxla*) and grows to a height of 15ft. (4.5m.) or more when the roots are confined to large pots. It is truly splendid when it takes on its more adult appearance, with large, arrow-shaped leaves on 2ft. (60cm.) long petioles (leaf stalks) attached to stout stems. Like the monstera, which belongs to the same family, the *Araceae*, it benefits from having a moss-covered support for the aerial roots to cling to. Indoors, one would not expect to have such majestic plants, but it is comforting to know that these plants do in fact grow, they don't just sit about getting more and more bedraggled as the days go on.

For the smaller apartment there is the Sweetheart Plant, *P. scandens*, which has green, heart-shaped leaves which are much smaller and on flexible stems which allows the growths to be trained to a trellis work support, so giving the plant a much fuller appearance.

There are dozens of other philodendrons which are all essentially foliage plants, but these contrast considerably in appearance – they are mostly in short supply and it would only cause frustration to mention their names here for they might well prove to be unobtainable. All of them require much the same treatment; i.e. warm conditions (moist if possible, and that may mean spraying the foliage periodically) and shade from direct sunlight. All of these are moisture lovers in their natural habitat, so it is important that they receive adequate moisture at their roots, but the pots must never be allowed to stand in water for any length of time. Large plants of the philodendron tribe will also require adequate feeding – a liquid fertiliser applied in small quantities but often is the best.

Phoenix (Date Palm)

These are coarse palms that develop substantial trunks in time, and don't show their true adult appearance until they are at least six years old. One of the most fascinating things about them is the way in which the new leaves, which are covered in a silvery down, unfold themselves. The two you are most likely to come across are *Phoenix canariensis* and *P. roebelenii*, the former being the more graceful of the two.

Clay pots suit them best, and a heavier compost mixture such as the John Innes No. 3 potting compost will be needed when potting, a task that must not be neglected. Their care amounts to providing them with a light position in a warm room which is well aired in hot-weather conditions, and watering that is at no time neglected, although less will be needed in winter. They seem to like large pots so don't be afraid to pot them on in early summer if their pots are well filled with roots. Cleaning the very narrow leaves is an almost impossible task, and is best done by hosing the plant over out of doors on a warm day.

Pilea

Nothing very splendid, the pileas are essentially 'in-filling' plants which are grown for their foliage. In their favour, they are easily managed and will adapt to all sorts of situations, provided they are given reasonable warmth and light shade. Cuttings root with no difficulty, so it is better to raise fresh plants annually rather than to attempt to persevere with rather battered old ones. *Pilea cadierei* has silvery foliage, but its smaller form *P. cadierei nana* is better, while *P. repens* is a species with lime-green leaf colouring. This last is commonly named Moon Valley. *P. involucrata* has the pleasant common name of Friendship Plant, and has a splash of silver colouring in the centre of an otherwise dull, blackish-coloured leaf. From the very insignificant flowers seed is produced which will result in young plants growing all over the place – an interesting prospect, perhaps, but it really is not a very pleasing plant to have around. Average conditions out of bright sunlight suit all the pileas.

Pineapple, see Ananas

Plectranthus

The plectranthus is a simple sort of plant which is usually acquired by getting a few cuttings from a friend and inserting them in almost any reasonable compost mixture in order to get them under way. With no special attention other than keeping them warm and moist they will grow at a remarkable rate, and are possibly seen to best effect when planted in hanging baskets that are suspended in a window area offering reasonable light.

Plectranthus australis has small, rounded, attractive glossy green leaves with crenate margins which are borne on succulent stems, and *P. oertendhalii* has less glossy leaves that are, however, attractively veined. No special cultural advice is needed as this must be one of the easiest possible plants to care for.

Pleomele reflexa variegata (Song of India)

We have some of these in the greenhouses that are over 20 years old and are looked upon as family treasures, as they are well-nigh irreplaceable. Commonly named Song of India, the Pleomele belongs to the same family as the dracaenas, the *Liliaceae*, and has the typical strong stem of the taller-growing dracaenas, but its leaves are very much shorter. These leaves are a rich yellow in colour with a faint green stripe and, being closer together on the stem than is the case of the dracaenas, they are foliage plants with few peers. They are, in fact, one of my especial favourites. Not desperately difficult to grow, they require good light and reasonable warmth with fairly dry conditions at their roots, particularly in the winter months. *Pleomele reflexa variegata*, with superb golden foliage, is the one to go for. The green form isn't worth bothering about.

Plumbago capensis (Cape Leadwort)

Although it is not really a house plant, unless you are particularly capable, *Plumbago capensis* is an excellent climber for the cool conservatory or greenhouse. It bears masses of striking pale blue flowers throughout the summer months. Even the cool porch area is a possibility if the plant can be provided with a minimum temperature of around 7.5°C. (45°F.) during the winter months, and it is not exposed to too much direct sun at other times. Provide a frame for the growths to be attached to, water and feed during the summer months and then keep on the dry side with no feeding in winter.

Poinsettia

Commercial establishments normally take cuttings of the Poinsettia (*Euphorbia pulcherrima*) during the early part of the summer in order to have plants ready for the Christmas rush. And in recent years there has been a tremendous rush as these plants have steadily gone up the popularity charts. Like the hibiscus, they have really come into their own as a result of growth-retarding chemicals, which keep the plants short and compact, rather than long and leggy as would be the case if they were grown naturally without the regular applications of such chemicals.

Once rooted they are potted, mostly, into 5in. (13cm.) pots, and grown on in greenhouses that offer maximum light and temperatures that do not fall below 17°C. (62°F.). With proper feeding and regular watering plants are in full flower during their natural flowering time, which is December. The flowers, in fact, form a very insignificant cluster in the centre of the colourful bracts at the top of the main stems and it is these which are the main attraction. Bracts are the topmost leaves which turn colour as the day-length shortens, and may be red, pink, white or multi-coloured. When buying plants, seek out compact, sturdy specimens with dark green leaves, and avoid the leggy ones with a washed-out, yellow appearance. Full light is most essential once they are indoors, and care must be taken not to water excessively. Feed with weak liquid fertiliser.

It is not unusual to have plants (even indoors) with colourful bracts for six months or more, but it is more likely that after about three months the leaves will begin to yellow and fall off, and this will be followed by the bracts discolouring and following the example set by the leaves. This natural function of the plant must be taken as a warning that it is in need of very much less water, no more feeding, and will benefit from resting with the compost almost dry for six to eight weeks. When most of the leaves and bracts have been shed the plant can be cut back to within a few inches of the top of the compost.

Euphorbia pulcherrima (**Poinsettia**).

Following the dormant period you will see leaf buds forming at the nodes (joints) where the leaves were previously attached to the plant, and this should be a signal that, gradually, more water is needed. This is also the signal that the plants should be knocked from their pots and some of the old compost removed before repotting into a slightly larger container. Use John Innes No. 3 potting compost to which a little extra peat has been added.

From then onwards a light and sunny windowsill is again the best position, and when the new shoots have attained a height of some 4in. (10cm.) it will be beneficial to remove their growing points. This will keep the plant reasonably compact, but I doubt very much if it will ever regain the appearance it had when you bought it. And it is a debatable question whether it will ever again bear bright and colourful bracts. Most of the experts say it is impossible, but I have known them to be successfully brought into colour for a second time indoors. The most important requirement (having kept the plant in good order!) is to ensure that from about the end of September onwards the plant should be exposed only to natural daylight, as any additional artificial light in the evening will simply encourage it to produce new leaves.

Primrose, Cape, see Streptocarpus

Primula

The extensive primula family provides us with many fine potted plants that will do well in cool, light and airy conditions once they are taken into the home. They also need adequate watering, and will usually be the better for having their pots plunged in a larger container filled with moist peat, wet moss, or even wet newspaper. A collection of several plants grown in this way in a larger container can provide a very pleasing feature – and so grown the plants will perform infinitely better.

Plants may be raised from seed, but this is a fiddling business and it is often better to begin by purchasing young plants that are already rooted and gradually pot them on into slightly larger pots. Even if established young plants are bought, they will do very much better if they are potted on into slightly larger pots as soon as you get them home. I know that most books go through a lengthy rigmarole about the best times to pot and the fatal consequences that will result if these directions are not followed – much of it is eyewash and plants don't read books, they simply like to have some fresh nourishing mixture around their roots when these have filled the pots they are growing in at the time.

Primula obconica is the species with larger than normal leaves which will flower almost throughout the year if the flower heads are removed as they fade (its main season is late winter and spring); but it has a nasty side to its character and contact with its leaves can cause very painful irritation to anyone with sensitive skin. Suspect this plant as the culprit if skin problems follow its introduction to the home. It can cause a severe rash if you are allergic to it. The late winter and spring flowering *P. malacoides* is an altogether neater and more attractive plant with the daintiest of flowers, borne in whorls up the stems, in all the pastel shades imaginable. A group of these placed together will give pleasure for many months.

Red-hot Cat's Tail, see Acalpha

Rhoeo discolor (Three Men in a Boat, Moses in the Bulrushes)

Moist, shaded and warm conditions are needed for this member of the tradescantia, or *Commelineae*, family, which have two common names, Three Men in a Boat and Moses in the Bulrushes. The first name alludes to the fact that the flower resembles a boat and the stamens three men sitting in it – perhaps I am either stupid or have the wrong sort of plant, but I can never see this sort of resemblance. Still, it's a nice thought!

There is a green form, but the most interesting and colourful rhoeo is *Rhoeo discolor* which forms rosettes of lance-shaped leaves which are burgundy-red on the reverse and a brownish-green and cream on the upper surface. To propagate, simply place a mature plant in flower on a tray of peat and allow the seed to fall naturally to germinate in the peat. The resulting plants can be removed when large enough to handle. Rhoeos may also be increased by dividing the older clumps, which is best for *R. discolor*.

Rhoicissus (Grape Ivy)

Recently, in *Rhoicissus Ellendanica*, we have seen an improvement on the old-established and very tough *R. rhomboidea*. The newly introduced one has a serrated edge to the leaves and is most attractive. With glossy tri-lobed leaves, the Grape Ivies are among the easiest of plants to grow and will tolerate darker conditions better than almost any of the other modern house plants. They may be used as trailing plants, but these natural climbers are at their best when covering a framework, or when attached to a stout stake.

Although they do reasonably well in darker positions, they will be more compact and attractive growing where the conditions are lighter, though not sunny. Keep them moist, well fed and pot them on as they outgrow their existing pots, using a peaty compost mixture.

Saintpaulia (African Violet)

In Germany Saintpaulias are commonly named Usambara Violets, which refers to the mountainous region of East Africa from where the cultivated varieties originally derived, but we settle for the simpler term, African Violet. At flower shows I like to think that our saintpaulias are the best in the tent, hall or wherever. And we don't do so badly – the larger plants, if placed in the centre of an L.P., would completely cover the record with their leaves, and the centre of the plants would be completely filled with sparkling fresh flowers.

We do it by taking individual leaf cuttings, inserting them in peat with a little sand added, and giving them the benefit of temperatures that do not fall below 21°C. (70°F.). You can get reasonable results with lower temperatures, but reasonable results are not good enough when every cutting counts. Once the cuttings are well rooted and producing small leaves, the leaves are removed from the propagating material and the clusters of plantlets around the leaf stalk are teased apart so that we are left with tiny individual plantlets each with two small leaves of their own and a few wispy roots. These go into shallow boxes filled with peat mixture, in which they will be grown on in the same high temperature. The reason for teasing the young plants apart is to ensure that each plant as it develops has only one central growing point from which all leaves will radiate. And the reason for wanting that sort of plant is to ensure that it will develop with its leaves lying more or less flat on top of the pot and the flowers standing proudly away from them. The alternative to that would be to plant the entire clump from the base of the parent leaf but this would result in a messy plant with leaves and flowers poking out in all directions.

With plants in the home it is essential that they should be in light positions, and fairly sunny spots will not be detrimental provided you are careful not to get water on to the leaves and flowers. It will also help the plants if additional artificial light is provided in the evenings by locating them under a table or wall light. It is frequently recommended that they should be watered with tepid water, and this is advisable, but I was completely knocked off my stride one evening when addressing a horticultural society when someone asked where they could purchase tepid water! Tepid water doesn't mean boiling kettles so that the poor plants are scalded, it simply means that the water should have the chill taken off it. Water should either be directed into the pot with a watering can, or the plants should be placed in a saucer of water and allowed to take up all they require by capillary action. Never leave them standing in water once they have obviously taken up all they need. Established plants can be fed with a weak dilution of liquid fertiliser each time they are watered, but it is only necessary to feed in winter if the plants are obviously putting on growth.

Too-frequent potting on of African Violets is quite unnecessary and could well do more harm than good. But when the plant has been carefully knocked from its pot and is seen to have matted roots all around the compost, then potting can be contemplated. It is best to use shallow pots, and they should be only slightly larger than the one in which the plant is growing at present. The potting mixture should be very much on the peaty side.

As individual flowers die off they should be removed, and when there are no flowers left on the flower stalk the stalk should be completely removed, no pieces being left attached to the plant – if left they are likely to rot and damage the remainder of the plant. Leaves should be removed in the same way when they have lost their colour or are badly marked. Dead flowers and leaves do nothing whatsoever for any plant and are best in the dustbin.

There is considerable variation in the quality of plants offered for sale – and not only in the quality of growth, but also in constitution. Plant hybridists are continually introducing plants that are more floriferous, more disease resistant and better able to withstand the strain of home conditions, once they have left the tender care of the experienced grower at the nursery. So it is well to look out for these stronger plants when making purchases. Reject sick and weedy plants with drooping leaves for these are not likely to improve once they have been taken home. Go back another day if you cannot find the plants you want – ones with rich green, firm leaves, and strong-stemmed flowers which also have a fresh appearance.

I'm frequently asked by people who have bought plants with several crowns producing flowers and leaves all over the place, if these can be split up (as I remarked a little earlier it is this kind of formation which it is best to avoid). The answer is that you can, but the results are seldom very satisfactory. It is better to begin at the beginning and start with new plants produced from the many leaf cuttings that will be available.

Sansevieria trifasciata laurentii (Mother-in-Law's Tongue)

Mother-in-Law's Tongue is the common name of the most important of the sansevierias, *Sansevieria trifasciata laurentii*. This is as tough as old boots and will give no trouble provided it is kept warm, very much on the dry side and in good light. Feeding is not necessary and potting on is done when the plant breaks the pot in which it is growing. Use a heavy compost mixture when potting. There are numerous other sansevierias that are sometimes available, and all will respond well to somewhat spartan treatment. New plants are made from the young plants which develop beside the parent plants, and these can be cut away and rooted at any time.

176

Sansevieria trifasciata laurentii **(Mother-in-Law's Tongue).**

Saxifraga sarmentosa (Mother of Thousands)

Saxifraga sarmentosa has numerous common names but Mother of Thousands is probably the most appropriate, and refers to the numerous plantlets that hang down from the parent plant on thin, trailing stems. These will provide you with new plants without difficulty, when detached. This easily managed plant will do well when suspended in some form of hanging pot in a light window position, and it needs moist soil, occasional feeding and reasonable warmth.

Schefflera digitata (Umbrella Plant)

The schefflera is one of the many plants that seem to have the confusing name of Umbrella Plant as a common appendage. In *Schefflera digitata*, large, digitate green leaves are well spaced out on stout stems which do not normally need stakes to support them. A substantial tree in the tropics, this schefflera will attain a height in excess of 15ft. (4.5m.) when the roots are confined to a large pot. Spacious surroundings are necessary, with reasonable warmth and shade from direct sunlight. Keep the soil moist and feed once the plant is well established. When necessary, the leaves should be cleaned with a damp sponge or soft cloth.

Schlumbergera gaertneri (Whitsun Cactus)

There are several varieties of the Whitsun Cactus *Schlumbergera gaertneri* (it is also known as *Epiphyllopsis gaertneri* and *Rhipsalidopsis gaertneri*) that differ mainly in the colour of their elongated trumpet-shaped flowers. These are shades of red and appear in spring. New plants are easily raised from the leaf pads that form in sections. These plants must be given a light window position, and they should never be allowed to become too wet at the roots. Also, once they have set flowers it is better to leave the plants in the same position and not to move them about the room to obtain a more pleasing effect. Putting them out in a sunny, sheltered position in the garden in summer will do them no harm, and may improve their chances of flowering more freely.

Scindapsus aureus (Money Plant or Devil's Ivy)

The variety with almost white leaves marked with a few green patches is *Scindapsus aureus* Marble Queen and is almost impossible to grow well. It is an ideal subject for the moist confines of a growing case. The best scindapsus to grow is the species *aureus* itself, which has golden leaf variegation and which does amazingly well when grown by the Hydroculture method (see p. 185). In any event, scindapsuses require moist, shaded conditions and compost that is never allowed to dry out. They will climb or trail and, being aeroids, when encouraged to climb they should be provided with a mossed support.

Screw Pine, see Pandanus

Scindapsus aureus (**Money Plant or Devil's Ivy**).

Sensitive Plant, see Mimosa pudica

Sinningia, see Gloxinia

Shrimp Plant, see Beloperone guttata

Slipper Flower, see Calceolaria

Solanum capsicastrum (Winter Cherry)

The Winter Cherry, *Solanum capsicastrum*, has rather hard green-coloured leaves, and produces attractive orange-red berries at Christmas as well as at other times of the year. The most important cultural requirement is for it to be given the lightest possible place in which to grow, as the berries will quickly drop in dark positions – they are prone to do this in more favourable positions on dull days. Water frequently and feed well.

Song of India, see Pleomele reflexa variegata

Sparmannia africana (African Wind Flower, Indoor Lime)

The African Wind Flower and Indoor Lime are two of the common names of *Sparmannia africana,* the second of these referring to the attractive lime-green colouring of the large, rather coarse leaves. Umbels of white flowers are borne in May and June, the pistils of which open outwards whenever there is a movement of air, hence the reason for its other common name. This is a free-growing plant that needs ample space in which to develop, but pruning at almost any time will present few problems. Water, feed well and pot on annually into a slightly heavy compost mixture when the pot in which the plant is growing becomes filled with roots. Eventually, it can progress to a pot of 10in. (25cm.) size and after that it can be kept in good health by regular feeding. It is a favourite plant of mine but it never seems to get anywhere in the popularity stakes.

Spathiphyllum (White Sails)

There are two spathiphyllums, the smaller of these being *Spathiphyllum wallisii* which has dull green leaves and insignificant white flowers, and needs ample moisture, warmth and shade to have a chance of survival. Much superior is *S.* Mauna Loa with much bolder leaves and splendid white flower-like spathes that stand well away from the broadly lance-shaped leaves, but it is not easily obtainable. As it makes more vigorous growth, the latter needs more frequent potting on, and a heavy compost with peat worked into it is suitable. This needs similar conditions to *S. wallisii.*

Spider Plant, see Chlorophytum comosum

Stephanotis floribunda (Madagascar Jasmine)

Stephanotis floribunda is a marvellous plant which bears clusters of white flowers with a fragrance that will permeate every corner of the room. These are borne against a background of dark green, evergreen foliage. But it isn't easy to grow; in fact, it can prove a great problem for most people who try to make a room plant of it. In the greenhouse it does better, but if you have to grow it in the home throughout the year then it must be given very good light and must not be excessively watered at any time, particularly in winter. During the winter months the loss of some leaves will be inevitable, but you should not try to remedy this by watering the plant as this is only likely to aggravate the problem. The vigorous growths need a framework to support them. A special watch must be kept among the twining stems and the leaves for mealy bugs, for these find the stephanotis a pleasing host.

Streptocarpus (Cape Primrose)

We have seen many new streptocarpus hybrids introduced in recent years, but I still prefer the old *Streptocarpus* Constant Nymph with its masses of colourful blue flowers, produced throughout the summer months above bold foliage. Good light but shade from strong sunshine and modest warmth with regular watering and feeding will keep all the Cape Primroses, as they are called, in good fettle. They are easy enough to propagate by cutting up the very stiff, unbending leaves and placing the pieces upright or on the flat in boxes filled with fresh peat.

Sweetheart Plant, see Philodendron scandens

Swiss Cheese Plant, see Monstera

Three Men in a Boat, see Rhoeo discolor

Thunbergia alata (Black-eyed Susan)

A simple common name, Black-eyed Susan, and pretty orange flowers with jet black centres (borne in summer) would seem to be the reason for this plant's success! Thunbergia alata forms a mass of climbing and twining stems which bear small and dreary leaves that are in themselves something of a disaster. But this is a popular plant, and the care it needs is very much the norm for indoor flowering plants: reasonable light and warmth, reasonable amounts of moisture at the roots and regular feeding. Keep a careful eye open for pests as this plant seems to attract a wide selection.

Tillandsia cyanea

The tillandsias are mostly plants for the enthusiast who can appreciate their finer points and is able to pay the rather high asking price for what, at first sight, seems very little. These compact little plants belong to the *Bromeliaceae* family and grow very much better when attached to a mossed bromeliad 'tree'. Most of them will flower reasonably well and, though small, the flowers are a startling blue colour. They need to be kept warm, and in light shade, and when attached to a piece of bark or old tree stump with moss around their roots they seem able to go for months without water. Feeding is not necessary.

Tillandsia cyanea forms clumps of narrow greenish-brown leaves from which develop cerise-coloured bracts of cuttlefish shape, and from which in turn arise the blue flowers.

Tradescantia fluminensis (Wandering Sailor)

The tradescantias are among the most humble of house plants, but they are among my favourites as they offer so much in return for, usually, very little care. Light shade, cool and airy conditions and a reasonable amount of watering and feeding would seem to sum up their needs. There are lots of different leaf colours, with the silver, reddish-brown and golden being best. The majority are varieties of the trailing *Tradescantia fluminensis*, with the silver-variegated variety Quicksilver being one of the most showy. Cuttings a few inches in length will root at any time of the year.

These tradescantias are fine as basket plants, hanging pot plants and edging plants. You should always have a few around.

Umbrella Plant, see Schefflera digitata

Urn Plant, see Aechmea

Venus's Fly Trap, see Dionaea muscipula

Violet, Africa, see Saintpaulia

Vriesia

Generally available is *Vriesia splendens* which forms a rosette
of patterned, recurring leaves and bears a splendid-looking,
spear-shaped bract of bright red colouring. Keep this plant
warm and lightly shaded, and water by filling the central urn
(formed by the rosette of leaves) as necessary.

The striking and much bolder species *V. fenestralis* and *V.
hieroglyphica* are seldom heard of because they take a very long
time to develop and so are not commercially viable. If you ever
visit the greenhouses of one of the better botanic gardens,
however, it is more than likely that you will be able to see them
there. Both form splendid rosettes of arching leaves and flower
in about their tenth year – but it is the leaves which are the
attraction for the flowers, alas, are not much to write home
about.

Wandering Jew, see Zebrina pendula

Wandering Sailor, see Tradescantia fluminensis

Wax Plant, see Hoya

White Sails, see Spathiphyllum

Whitsun Cactus, see Schlumbergera gaertneri

Winter Cherry, see Solanum capsicastrum

Zebrina pendula (Wandering Jew)

The zebrinas are very similar to the tradescantias, but have
broader leaves. Those of *Zebrina pendula* (Wandering Jew) are

a lovely burgundy shade on the reverse side and have silver markings on the upper surface.

The zebrinas make marvellous basket plants and *Z. pendula* has a variety named Quadricolor with rose-purple, white striped leaves; coloured purple on the underside. *Z. purpusii* with purple, flushed green leaves, also purple on the underside, makes a splendid basket plant if several potsful of smaller plants are put in the basket at the outset – they seldom do much if a single plant is put in at the beginning. Care for them in the same way as the tradescantias.

Zygocactus truncatus (Christmas Cactus)

The zygocactus is another cactus that forms pads of growths one on the end of the other, and, if you are lucky, about Christmas time, *Zygocactus truncatus* (called the Christmas Cactus) may even form attractive reddish-orange flowers on the ends of the pads themselves. Whether the flowers arrive before, at or after that time depends to a large extent on the room temperature – the higher it is, the sooner they will flower. Put the plants outside in a sheltered, sunny place during the summer and keep them on a sunny windowsill at other times. Keep them reasonably warm and avoid excessive watering.

CHAPTER TEN

The Future is Already Here

As far as plants go I am a bit of a stick-in-the-mud. Anything too radical in the way of cultivation I look on with the utmost scepticism, a trait no doubt inherited from my Granny who was a very canny Scot. The trouble is that I have met far too many intensely enthusiastic people over the years with ambitious, revolutionary ideas that have seldom got off the ground.

So when, one day, a man handed me a pot full of stones with a plant growing out of the middle, and more or less said, that all that was needed was a few inches of water and his magical new fertiliser to make it prosper, I thought to myself, 'Here we go again.' But he was right, my suspicious Scottish mind was soon won over to this revolutionary method of growing plants – indeed, I had no alternative as the majority of plants that were tested seemed to grow fantastically well. In particular, plants of the aeroid family – monsteras, philodendrons and anthuriums – did especially well. They revelled in the ever-present oxygen and moisture at their roots. These are moisture-loving plants that do infinitely better when grown in conditions of high humidity, which means that they must be provided with warmth as well as moisture. However, in the case of anthuriums, in particular, there is a marked tendency for conventional compost mixtures to become waterlogged from too much watering, which in turn reduces the amount of oxygen around the roots of the plant. When there is no oxygen, the roots have little chance of survival and the plant begins to deteriorate, and the anthurium is by no means alone when it comes to suffering in this way.

This new system is called Hydroculture and it works in the

following way. At the nursery, although cuttings can be rooted in water quite successfully, the general practice is to start the plant off in conventional fashion by rooting the cutting or sowing the seed in a peat and sand mixture and then potting the young plant into an appropriate potting mixture. Having become reasonably established the plant is then taken from its pot and every vestige of soil is removed, because if any were left it would almost certainly create problems of toxicity at a later date.

The next step is to hold the plant centrally in a special Hydroculture growing pot while Hydroleca granules are poured in around the exposed roots. Tapping the pot on the bench settles the granules, there being no need to firm them in position. Tall growing plants are given supporting stakes which are placed in the pot at this early stage, as it becomes very difficult to perform this task once the pot has been filled with granules.

Once potted, the plant is taken to a specially constructed greenhouse bench and stood in about 3in. (8cm.) of water. The water drains through a sump hole at one end of the bench and is then re-circulated by means of a pump which continually replenishes the supply of water at the opposite end of the bench. Water is returned through pressure jets that ensure there is ample oxygen in the supply of water – an essential factor if the beds of water are to remain free of algae that would in time be harmful to developing plants.

After the conversion from soil to granules, it takes some three months before the plant is considered sufficiently established to be removed from the bed of flowing water and placed in the sort of container in which you will grow the plant in your home. One of the factors that helped win me over to growing plants in this way is the incredible root systems that such plants are able to develop – these were clearly much stronger and more vigorous than the root systems of similar plants growing in soil. During their time on the greenhouse benches, the plants are provided with nutrients at predetermined levels that are regularly checked to ensure that no imbalance occurs.

Leca is a trade name coined from the initial letters of Lightest

Expanded Clay Aggregate, which is used in the building industry to make light-weight concrete. Hydroleca is made from the same London blue clay which is baked in an oven at high temperature before being transformed into the granules that have the appearance of irregular-shaped Maltesers. The composition is also very similar in that the pebbles have a dense outer surface with a honeycomb centre.

The granules hold about one-third of their own weight of water, which is an important cultural factor, and the Hydroleca grade of pebble is much smaller than the one used for making concrete. The smaller granule provides better support for the plant, and ensures much better capillary action within the pot. Other materials may also be used for supporting the plant, but the baked clay granules have proved to be by far the most effective. Besides their usefulness in this repect, I find the wetted granules extremely useful in plant arrangements – the soft brown colouring provides an excellent foil for plants and is ideal for creating pathways and open areas that give a lightness to one's work.

Besides advances with water culture in relation to potted plants there has also been considerable progress with edible crops using what is known as the nutrient film technique, NFT, which entails suspending plants over a canal of moving water, but it is very much a professionally controlled operation that would be quite beyond the scope of the ordinary amateur gardener. And to have, on a windowsill, potted plants which require constant monitoring to ensure that they are getting the required amount of nutrient would be out of the question as few of us have either the time or the expertise to make this possible. Here, however, the most important step of all was made by the Bayer Chemical Company of Germany, who developed their ion fertiliser added at shorter intervals than the supplier recommends.

Although plants grown by the Hydroculture method should be cared for in exactly the same way as conventional plants in respect of positioning, pest control and so on, there is one thing which has to be taken account of. The temperature of the water is lower than that of the surrounding air and for this reason it is vital to grow Hydroculture plants in a room with a minimum temperature of 16°C. (60°F.), with 18.5°C. (65°F.) being preferable.

At first there was a tendency for owners of Hydroculture plants to be forever topping up the water level in the container. This reduces the oxygen around the roots and invites rotting. So it is important to fill the container to the 'maximum' mark on the water level gauge and to allow the level to drop to the 'minimum' mark and remain there for five to seven days before re-filling. As already mentioned, it is essential to use tap water in preference to rain water or water from a well.

Unless plants increase in size so much that they are out of proportion to the containers in which they are growing, there should be no need to transfer them to larger containers, provided you do not neglect feeding. If it is necessary to transfer a plant, it should be removed from its inner pot (the roots will hold most of the Hydroleca together) and placed in a larger one, filling in all the empty spaces in the pot with Hydroleca as the operation progresses. A larger outer container will also be necessary, but this is no great problem as almost anything will do from a bucket to a dustbin, provided it is watertight.

A new water-level indicator may be needed; if so, it should register some 3in. (8cm.) of water from the bottom of the pot upwards, as this is the amount of water required around the roots of the plant. The 'minimum' mark should allow the water to fall to the base of the pot. But I don't find in practice that it is necessary to be too fussy about water indicators. My splendid plant of *Heptapleurum arboricola* is in a smallish Hydroculture growing pot which simply stands in a slightly wider decorative pot with no Hydroleca filling between the pots, and there is no water indicator whatsoever. But don't discount the canny Scottish eye that periodically peeps down between the outer and inner containers to check the water level. The excellent condition of the plant leaves no doubt in my mind that this rather crude method of checking the water level works perfectly.

You should put a small sticker on the side of the container recording the date on which the next feed is due, but I find that my heptapleurum tells me when feeding is necessary.

When the topmost leaves take on a slightly paler colour, I know that another packet of fertiliser is required.

The vigorous growth of many Hydroculture plants is often quite astounding, which is one good reason for ensuring that they are not exposed to excessive sunlight, as the more lush foliage will suffer more readily than that on the conventionally-grown plant. There are one or two plants that are obviously not entirely happy when growing in this way, but the vast majority, including the sansevieria, which loves dry conditions, and many cacti seem to revel in it. Flowering plants have not yet been seriously considered for this method of culture as it is felt that the more expensive Hydroculture plant should be of a more permanent nature. But that is not to say that flowering plants will not do well and one of the most popular of them, the saintpaulia, flourishes in the conditions that Hydroculture offers.

Landscaping of office interiors with foliage plants grown by this method has probably been the most successful of all aspects of their culture. I know a florist who turns down offers of landscaping jobs if it is insisted that the plants should be grown conventionally in compost. And for a florist to turn down business because he cannot have his own way suggests that there really is a great future for plants grown by this method.

The precise shape and size of these larger office planters does not make much difference, provided they are watertight. But it is important that they should be level, and it is preferable that they should not be too massive in size, as there will surely come the time when the container has to be moved around, or emptied for some reason or other. Containers that are too deep do little for the appearance of the plants growing in them, and simply mean that an unnecessary amount of Hydroleca has to be used to fill them up.

When planting, the required amount of fertiliser is first placed in the bottom of the container, and then enough Hydroleca is added to bring the growing pot to just below the rim of the container when it is standing on the surface of the Leca. It is essential that all the pots being placed in the container should be the same depth, and that the base of the water-level indicator is on the same level as the bottom of the growing pots.

Having positioned the plants and the indicator the spaces between the pots are filled in with Leca granules, and there should be sufficient in the container to just cover the tops of the plant pots. The next step is to fill the container with water until it reaches the maximum level on the gauge. Topping up may be necessary after a short time to compensate for the amount of water absorbed by the Leca granules.

The Leca granules are very dusty when purchased, and it is essential that they should be hosed clean before being introduced into the container. Failure to do so will result in the dust particles gathering around the base of the indicator and preventing it functioning properly.

I've said that the future is here already, but there is clearly still much to be learned about this fascinating method of growing plants. Whether it will ever completely oust the conventional medium of compost is a matter for conjecture, but if the office landscaping scene is anything to go by, we may well see yet another potted-plant revolution before we are very much older.

Hydroculture, nevertheless, is only one aspect of the work that is being done by nurserymen and others to produce something new, something different, and something better in the way of pot plants for the home. A tremendous amount of research and experimentation has, of course, already contributed much to the range of house plants available, but the multitude of new things that continue to appear never ceases to amaze me – the better varieties of saintpaulia being just one example; better poinsettias; better ficuses (notably *Ficus* Europa); *Heptapleurum arboricola* and its forms, and *Dracaena marginata tricolor*. All of these are rather remarkable plants which have added much to the house plant scene, and they are, of course, discussed elsewhere in these pages.

Surprisingly, not all new plant introductions of promise are seized upon by the house-plant grower. Some unusual and distinctive plants introduced over the years have met with resistance, and I am thinking particularly of the very fine *Beloperone lutea* which has yellow bracts as opposed to the orange-brown bracts of *B. guttata*. It has never really caught on and is now seldom offered as a pot plant.

The same might be said of the old *Aphelandra squarrose louisae* which, as I've mentioned on p. 107, is a plant that has almost become extinct, simply because it was thought that there were better plants following on. Now, we find that we might have been a bit hasty in our judgement, for the successors to *A. squarrosa louisae* have not really proved to be all that startling. It would seem, from my experience, that the house plant grower and his customers are very conservative in their taste. For example, Hydroculture took a long time to become accepted, but now that it has, it is proving to be extremely successful. That is how it usually is in the world of plants.

Naturally, as production costs increase, so plants become more expensive and this has given rise to increasing numbers of small plants being offered for sale. These are known as 'bottle garden' plants, and although they are not all necessarily suitable for bottle gardens, they are given this name because they are all small and in relatively tiny pots. In addition, they can be bought at relatively little cost. Almost immediately after purchase they can be potted into larger containers, and in time they will catch up on their big brothers. So you can build up a collection of plants most economically.

Index

Page numbers in italics indicate illustrations

Abutilon hybridum sativum, 84, 101
Acalypha, 84
  hispida, 102
  wilkesiana (*A. tricolor*), 102
Achimenes, 84, 102
Acorus gramineus, 84, 102
Adiantum, 84, 103
Aechmea, 84
  caudata, 104
  rhodocyanea (*A. fasciata*), *46*,
    103–4
Aeonium domesticum variegatum, 84,
  104
African Violet, *see* Saintpaulia
African Wind Flower, *see*
  Sparmannia africana
Agave americana, 84, *104*–5
Aglaonema, 85, 104
Allamanda neriifolia, 85, 105
Ananas, 85
  bracteatus striatus, 24–5, *25*, 106
Angel's Trumpets, *see* Datura
Anthurium, 85
  andreanum, 106
  hydroculture, 185
  scherzerianum, 106
Aphelandra, 44, 85
  squarrosa dania, 107
  s. louisae, 107, 191
Aralia sieboldii, 65, 85, *107*–8
Araucaria excelsa, 85, 108
Ardisia crispa, 85, 108
Asparagus, 86
  meyeri, 109
  plumosus, *108*–9
  sprengeri, 109
Aspidistra, 32, 49
  lurida, 86, 109, *109*
  propagation, 77

Asplenium nidus, 17–18, *18*, *33*,
  86, 110
autumn: presents for, 58–9
Azalea, 86, 110
  indica, 19–20, *20*, 55
  watering, 9
  water requirements, 66

Bamboo, *see* Bambusa
Bambusa, 86, 111
bathroom: plants for, 50
bedroom: plants for, 49–50
Begonia, 20–2, 86
  Fireglow, 44, 56–8
  fuchsioides, 113
  glaucophylla, 113
  haageana, 113
  lucerna, *113*–14
  maculata, 114
  manicata, 113
  masoniana, *112*–13
  pendulous, *111*–12
  Reiger, 112
  rex, *20*, *39*, 113
  richmondensis, 113
  semperflorens, 111
  tuberous, 111
Beloperone, 86
  guttata, 44, *45*, *114*–15, *114*
  pruning, 42
  lurea, 114, 190
  pruning, 6
Billbergia nutans, 86, 115
Bird's Nest Fern, *see* *Asplenium
  nidus*
Black-Eyed Susan, *see* Thunbergia
Bottle Brush, *see* Callistemon
Bougainvillea, 87, *115*–16
bowls: collection of plants in, 53

Bromeliads: after flowering, 7–8
Busy Lizzie, *see* Impatiens
buying plants, 12–13
  taking home, 52

Cacti, 48, *48*, 59, 87, 116–17
Caladium, 28, 87, 117–18
  candidum, 118
Calamondin Orange, *see Citrus
  mitis*
Calathea, 87, 118–19
  makoyana, 119
Calceolaria, 87, 119
Callistemon citrinus, 87, 119
Camellia, 87, 119–20
Campanula, 88
  isophylla, 120
  i. alba, 35
  pyramidalis, 120
Cape Jasmine, *see Gardenia
  jasminioides*
Cape Leadwort, *see Plumbago
  capensis*
Cape Primrose, *see* Streptocarpus
carboys, 37–9
care, 16, 61–73
Carex morrowii variegata, 88,
  120–21
Cast-iron Plant, *see* Aspidistra
Cephalocereus senilis, 15
Ceropegia woodii, 88, 121
chemicals: use, 68, 71
Chenille Plant, *see* Acalypha
Chlorophytum comosum, 33, *43*, 44,
  88, 121–2, *122*
  leaf browning, 8–9
  propagation, 77
Christmas Cactus, *see Zygocactus
  truncatus*
Chrysanthemum, 88, 122–3
Cigar Plant, *see* Cuphea
Cineraria, 88, 123
Cissus antarctica, *43*, 43–4, *45*, 88,
  123
Citrus mitis, 58–9, 88, 124
cleaning plants, 62–3
Clerodendrum thomsonae, 89, 124
Cliff Brake Fern, *see* Pellaea
Clivia miniata, 89, 124–5
Clog Plant, *see* Hypocyrta
Cocos weddelliana, 89, 125
Codiaeum, 14, 47–8, 56, 89, 125–6
Coffea arabica, 89, 126
Coffee Plant, *see Coffea arabica*

Coleus, 89, 126
  from seed, 74–6
Columnea, 15, 35, 89
  banksii, 127, *127*
  crassifolia (Firecracker), 127
compost: for plant cases, 37–8
conditions:
  finding right place, 27–50
  optimum, 63–4
  requirements, 16
consultant, 1–9
containers:
  depth in relation to plant size,
    53
  size in relation to plant, 71–3
  to stand in fireplace, 30–1
Cordyline terminalis, *see Dracaena
  terminalis*
Crassula argentea, 89, 128
Crossandra infundibuliformis, 90,
  128
Croton, *see* Codiaeum
Crown of Thorns, *see Euphorbia
  splendens*
Cryptanthus, 33, 90, 128–9, *129*
Cuphea platycentra (*C. ignea*), 90,
  130
cuttings, 76–7
Cyclamen, *20*, 22, 48, *48*, 60, 63,
  130–31
  persicum, 90
  reviving, 64
  watering, 3
Cyperus, 90
  alternifolius, 131
  diffusus, 131

Date Palm, *see* Phoenix
Datura suaveolens, 90, 132
Devil's Ivy, *see Scindapsus aureus*
Dieffenbachia, 90, 132–3
  amoena, 133
  exotica, 14, 133
dining-room: plants for, 45–8
Dionaea muscipula, 37, 133
Dipladenia splendens, 90, 133–4
dividing plants, 77
Dizygotheca elegantissima, 91, 134
Dracaena, 91
  deremensis, 15, 44, *45*, 134
  fragrans, 134–5
  godseffiana, *33*, 44
  Florida Beauty, 27, 135
  marginata, 15, 49

Red Edge, *46*, 135
 terminalis, 15, 44, *45*, 135
draughts, 68
Dumb Cane, *see* Dieffenbachia

Earth Star, *see* Cryptanthus
easy plants, 13–14
Echeveria, 91, 135–6
 retusa, *135*
Echinocactus grusonii, 91, 137–8,
 137
environment: creating, 37–9
Epiphyllopsis gaertneri, see
 Schlumbergera gaertneri
Epiphyllum, 91, 138
Episcia dianthiflora, 35, 91, 138
Eucalyptus, 91
 globulus, 139
 gunnii, 139
Euonymus japonicus aureovariegatus,
 91, 139
Euphorbia pulcherrima (Poinsettia),
 11, 44–5, 60, 97, 170–2, *171*
 splendens, 91, 139–40
Exacum affine, 92, 140

Fatshedera lizei, 92, 140
Fatsia japonica, see Aralia sieboldii
feeding:
 after repotting, 63, 80–1
 dangers of overfeeding, 64
 regular, 63–4
ferns, 15, 50
Ficus, 92, 140–4
 benjamina, 49, *143*, 143–4
 overwatering, 65
elastica (Rubber Plant), 11–12, 36
 leaves falling, 5
 e. decora, 11–12, 141
 e. d. tricolor, 143
 e. doescheri, 143
 e. robusta, 12, 43, *43*, 141, *142*
 Europa, 58
 pumila, 18–19, *18*, 140–41
Fig, *see* Ficus
fireplace: standing plants in, 30, *31*
fish tank: as plant case, 37, *38*
Fittonia, 92
 argyroneura, 144
 verschaffeltii, *38*
Flamingo Plant, *see* Anthurium
foliage plants: pruning, 6
Fuchsia, 92, 144–5
fungicides: use, 68, 71

Gardenia jasminioides, 92, 145–6
Geranium, *see* Pelargonium
Gloxinia, 92, 146
Golden Barrel Cactus, *see* Echino-
 cactus grusonii
Grape Ivy, *see* Rhoicissus
greenfly, 68–9
greenhouses: miniature, 37
Grevillea robusta, 92, 146–7
Guzmania, 93
 lingulata minor, 147
 Orangeade, 147
Gynura, 93, 147

hall: plants for, 43–4
hanging planter, 59
hanging plants, 34–5
Hearts Entangled, *see* Ceropegia
Hedera (Ivy), 93, 148–9
 canariensis: brown leaves, 6–7
 c. variegata, *18*, 19, 56, *56*, 62,
  148
 cuttings, 76
 helix Gold Heart, 149
 h. Jubilee, 22–3, *24*
 h. Little Diamond, 149
Helxine soleirolii, 93, 149
Heptapleurum, 47, 93
 arboricola, *46*, 56, *57*, 150
Hibiscus, 93
 bud and flower drop, 6
 cooperi variegata, 23–4, *24*
 rosa-sinensis, 150–52, *151*
 light requirements, 40–41
Hippeastrum, 93, 152–3
holidays: plant care during, 8, 67–8
Hot-water Plant, *see* Achimenes
Howeia fosteriana, see Kentia
Hoya, 93
 bella, 153
 carnosa, 153
Hydrangea, 93
 macrophylla, 55, 153–4
Hydroculture, 54, 60, 185–90
Hydroleca, 187–8
Hypocyrta glabra, 94, 154
Hypoestes, 94
 sanguinolenta, 155

Impatiens, 55, 94
 wallerana sultanii, 155
Indoor Lime, *see Sparmannia*
 africana
insecticides: use, 71

Iresine herbstii, 94, 155
Isolepis gracilis, 94, 155–6
Ivy, *see* Hedera

Jade Plant, *see Crassula argentea*
Jasminum polyanthum, 94, 156
Joseph's Coat, *see* Codiaeum

Kaffir Lily, *see* Clivia
Kalamchoe, 94, 157
Kangaroo Vine, *see* Cissus
Kentia, 94
  fosteriana, 49, 50, 157–9, *158*
kitchen: plants for, 48
Ladder Fern, *see* Nephrolepis
ladybirds: pest control by, 69
leaf-cleaning chemicals, 62–3
leaves: cleaning, *81*, 82
Leca, 186–7
light: requirements, 29–30
lighting, 39–42
Lime, Indoor, *see Sparmannia africana*

Madagascar Jasmine, *see* Stephanotis
Maidenhair Fern, *see* Adiantum
Maranta, 94
  leuconeura erythrophylla, 159
  l. kerchoveana, 159
  makoyana, *see Calathea makoyana*
mealy bug, 69, 70
Medinilla magnifica, 95, 159
Mimosa pudica, 95, 160
Mind Your Own Business, *see* Helxine
mobile displays, 32
Money Plant, *see Scindapsus aureus*
Monstera, 95
  aerial roots, 5–6
  deliciosa, 25, 25–6, 46, 46–7, 55, 160–1
  hydroculture, 185
  leaf forms, 6
  pertusa borsigiana, 160–1
Moses in the Bulrushes, *see Rhoeo discolor*
moss, 31–2
Mother-in-Law's Tongue, *see* Sansevieria
Mother of Thousands, *see Saxifraga sarmentosa*
mould, 61

names, 10–12
Neanthe bella, *33*, *38*, 95, 161–2
Neoregelia, 95, 162
Nephrolepis, 32
  exaltata, 25, 26, 95, 162–3
Nephthytis: pruning, 6
Norfolk Island Pine, *see Araucaria excelsa*

offices: plants in, 189
Old Man's Cactus, *see Cephalocereus senilis*
Oplismenus hirtella variegatus, 95, 163
Opuntia microdasys, 95, 163–4
outdoors: pot plants in summer, 7, 42–3

Pandanus, 95
  sanderi, 164–5
  utilis, 164
  veitchii, 164
Paper Flower, *see* Bougainvillea
Parasol Plant, *see* Heptapleurum
Parlour Palm, *see Neanthe bella*
pedestals: plants on, 32–3
Pelargonium, 58, 96, 165–6
Pellaea rotundifolia, 96, 166
Pellionia daveauana, 96, 166
Peperomia, 96
  caperata, 47, 166–7
  hederaefolia, 47, 166–7
  magnoliaefolia, 48, *48*, 166–7
  for plant cases, 39
  sandersii, 48, *48*, 166–7
pesticides: use, 68
pests, 13
  control, 68–71
Philodendron, 96
  hastatum, 50, 59, 167
  hydroculture, 185
  pruning, 6
  scandens, 35, *45*, 50, *50*, 167
  tuxla, 167
Phoenix, 96
  canariensis, 168
  roebelenii, 168
Pilea, 96
  cadierei, 168–9
  cuttings, 76–7
  involucrata, 168–9
  repens, 168–9
Pineapple, *see* Ananas
plantlets: propagation from, 77

Platycerium: leaf cleaning, 82
Plectranthus, 35, 96
   australis, 169
   oertendhalii, 169
Ploemele reflexa variegata, 97, 169
Plumbago capensis, 97, 170
Poinsettia, 11, 44–5, 60, 97, 170–2, 171
Polyanthus, *see Primula polyantha*
polystyrene: granules in soil, 3–4
pot covers, 52
potting: compost for, 79
   time for, 7
potting on, 71–3, 78–81, 79
presents: plants as, 51–60
Primula, 44, 97, 172–3
   malacoides, 173
   obconica, 173
   polyantha (Polyanthus):
      reviving, 9
problems, 1–9
propagation:
   cuttings, 76–7
   division, 77
   plantlets, 77
   from seed, 74–6
pruning, 42
   time for, 6

questions and answers, 4–9

Red-hot Cat's Tail, *see Acalypha*
red spider mite, 61–2
repotting, 71–3
   time for, 7, 78
Rhipsalidopsis gaertneri, *see Schlumbergera gaertneri*
Rhoeo discolor, 97, 173
Rhoicissus, 97
   Ellandanica, 31, 174
   rhomboidea, 35, 45–6, 53
root mealy bug, 69–71
Rubber Plant, *see Ficus elastica*

Saintpaulia (African Violet), 23, 24, 38, 40, 58, 97, 174–6
   blowing on, 3
   dividing, 8
   flowering, 4–5
   leaf cleaning, 82
Sansevieria, 46, 59–60
   trifasciata laurentii, 45, 46, 98, 176–7, 177
   watering, 66

Saxifraga sarmentosa, 98, 177
   propagation, 77
scale insects, 61
Schefflera, 47
   digitata, 98, 177–8
Schlumbergera gaertneri, 28, 98, 178
Scindapsus aureus, 98, 178
Screw Pine, *see Pandanus*
Scriptus cernuus, *see Isolepis gracilis*
seed: growing plants from, 74–6
seedlings: potting up, 75–6
Sensitive Plant, *see Mimosa pudica*
Shrimp Plant, *see Beloperone*
Silk Oak, *see Grevillea*
Sinningia, *see Gloxinia*
sitting-room: plants for, 44–5
size, 36
Slipper Plant, *see Calceolaria*
Solanum capsicastrum, 98, 179–80
Song of India, *see Ploemele*
sooty mould, 61
Sparmannia africana, 99, 180
Spathiphyllum, 99
   Mauna Loa, 180
   propagation, 77
   wallisii, 180
spring: presents for, 55–6
Stephanotis floribunda, 99, 180–1
Streptocarpus, 99
   Constant Nymph, 181
summer: presents for, 56–8
sun scorch, 28–30
Swiss Cheese Plant, *see Monstera*

tea: watering with, 3
temperatures: requirements, 63
Three Men in a Boat, *see Rhoeo discolor*
Thunbergia alata, 99, 181–2
Tillandsia cyanea, 99, 182
top dressing, 81–2
Tradescantia, 33, 50, 50, 59
   cuttings, 77
   fluminensis, 99, 182
trailing plants, 34–5
tray: plants in, 32, 33

Umbrella Plant, *see Schefflera*
Urn Plant, *see Aechmea*

Venus's Fly Trap, *see Dionaea muscipula*

Vriesia, 99
  fenestralis, 183
  hieroglyphica, 183
  splendens, 46, 183

Wandering Jew, *see Zebrina pendula*
Wandering Sailor, *see Tradescantia
    fluminensis*
watering, 64–6
  amount required, 66
  method, 2

with tea, 3
Wax Plant, *see* Hoya
White Sails, *see* Spathiphyllum
Whitsun Cactus, *see Schlumbergera
    gaertneri*
Winter Cherry, *see Solanum
    capsicastrum*
winter: presents for, 59–60

Zebrina pendula, 45, 100, 183–4
Zygocactus truncatus, 27–8, 100, 184

Prices and postage and packing rates shown below were correct at the time of going to press.

FICTION

All prices shown are exclusive of postage and packing.

GENERAL FICTION

☐ THE AFFAIR OF NINA B.	Simmel	£1.20
☐ H.M.S. BOUNTY	John Maxwell	£1.00
☐ TY-SHAN BAY	R. T. Aundrews	95p
☐ A SEA CHANGE	Lois Gould	80p
☐ THE PLAYERS	Gary Brandner	95p
☐ MR. FITTON'S COMMISSION	Showell Styles	85p
☐ CRASH LANDING	Mark Regan	95p
☐ SUMMER LIGHTNING	Judith Richards	£1.00
☐ THE HALO JUMP	Alistair Hamilton	£1.00
☐ SUMMERBLOOD	Anne Rudeen	£1.25
☐ PLACE OF THE DAWN	Gordon Taylor	90p
☐ EARTHLY POSSESSIONS	Anne Tyler	95p
☐ THE MASTER MECHANIC	I. G. Broat	£1.50
☐ THE MEXICAN PROPOSITION (Western)	Matt Chisholm	75p

CRIME/THRILLER

☐ THE TREMOR OF FORGERY	Patricia Highsmith	80p
☐ STRAIGHT	Steve Knickmeyer	80p
☐ THE COOL COTTONTAIL	John Ball	80p
☐ JOHNNY GET YOUR GUN	John Ball	85p
☐ CONFESS, FLETCH	Gregory Mcdonald	90p
☐ THE TRIPOLI DOCUMENTS	Henry Kane	95p
☐ THE EXECUTION	Oliver Crawford	90p
☐ TIME BOMB	James D. Atwater	90p
☐ THE SPECIALIST	Jasper Smith	85p
☐ KILLFACTOR FIVE	Peter Maxwell	85p
☐ ROUGH DEAL	Walter Winward	85p
☐ THE SONORA MUTATION	Albert J. Elias	85p
☐ THE RANSOM COMMANDO	James Grant	95p
☐ THE DESPERATE HOURS	Joseph Hayes	90p
☐ THE MOLE	Dan Sherman	95p

NON-FICTION

☐ THE HAMLYN BOOK OF CROSSWORDS 1		60p
☐ THE HAMLYN BOOK OF CROSSWORDS 2		60p
☐ THE HAMLYN BOOK OF CROSSWORDS 3		60p
☐ THE HAMLYN BOOK OF CROSSWORDS 4		60p
☐ THE HAMLYN FAMILY GAMES BOOK	Gyles Brandreth	75p
☐ LONELY WARRIOR (War)	Victor Houart	85p
☐ BLACK ANGELS (War)	Rupert Butler	£1.00
☐ THE SUNDAY TELEGRAPH PATIO GARDENING BOOK	Robert Pearson	80p
☐ THE COMPLETE TRAVELLER	Joan Bakewell	£1.50
☐ RESTORING OLD JUNK	Michèle Brown	75p
☐ FAT IS A FEMINIST ISSUE	Susie Orbach	85p
☐ AMAZING MAZES 1	Michael Lye	75p
☐ GUIDE TO THE CHANNEL ISLANDS	Janice Anderson and Edmund Swinglehurst	90p
☐ THE STRESS FACTOR	Donald Norfolk	90p
☐ WOMAN × TWO	Mary Kenny	90p
☐ THE HAMLYN BOOK OF BRAINTEASERS AND MINDBENDERS	Ben Hamilton	85p
☐ THE HAMLYN CARTOON COLLECTION 2		70p
☐ WORLD WAR 3	edited by Shelford Bidwell	£1.25
☐ THE HAMLYN BOOK OF AMAZING INFORMATION		80p
☐ IN PRAISE OF YOUNGER MEN	Sandy Fawkes	85p
☐ THE HAMLYN FAMILY QUIZ BOOK		85p
☐ BONEY M	John Shearlaw and David Brown	90p
☐ KISS	John Swenson	90p
☐ CARING FOR CATS AND KITTENS	John Montgomery	95p
☐ PUDDINGS AND DESSERTS (500 Recipes)	Monica Mawson	85p
☐ THE HAMLYN PRESSURE COOKBOOK	Jane Todd	85p
☐ HINTS FOR MODERN COOKS	Audrey Ellis	£1.00

COOKERY

☐ MIXER AND BLENDER COOKBOOK	Myra Street	80p
☐ HOME BAKED BREADS AND CAKES	Mary Norwak	75p
☐ EASY ICING	Marguerite Patten	85p
☐ HOME MADE COUNTRY WINES		40p
☐ COMPREHENSIVE GUIDE TO DEEP FREEZING		40p
☐ COUNTRY FARE	Doreen Fulleylove	80p
☐ HOME PRESERVING AND BOTTLING	Gladys Mann	80p
☐ WINE MAKING AT HOME	Francis Pinnegar	80p

All these books are available at your local bookshop or newsagent, or can be ordered direct from the publisher. Just tick the titles you want and fill in the form below.

NAME...

ADDRESS ....

....

Write to Hamlyn Paperbacks Cash Sales, PO Box 11, Falmouth, Cornwall TR10 9EN
Please enclose remittance to the value of the cover price plus:

UK: 25p for the first book plus 10p per copy for each additional book ordered to a maximum charge of £1.05.

BFPO and EIRE: 25p for the first book plus 10p per copy for the next 8 books, thereafter 4p per book.

OVERSEAS: 40p for the first book and 12p for each additional book.

Whilst every effort is made to keep prices low it is sometimes necessary to increase cover prices and also postage and packing rates at short notice. Hamlyn Paperbacks reserve the right to show new retail prices on covers which may differ from those previously advertised in the text or elsewhere.